DOCTRINE MATTERS

DOCTRINE MATTERS

Gordon Kuhrt (ed.)

HODDER AND STOUGHTON
LONDON SYDNEY AUCKLAND

British Library Cataloguing in Publication Data
A catalogue record for this book is
available from the British Library.

ISBN 0-340-56898-4

Published by Hodder and Stoughton,
a division of Hodder and Stoughton Ltd,
Mill Road, Dunton Green, Sevenoaks, Kent TN13 2YA.
Editorial Office: 47 Bedford Square, London WC1B 3DP.

Typeset by Hewer Text Composition Services, Edinburgh.
Printed in Great Britain by Cox & Wyman Ltd, Reading, Berks.

Contents

Foreword

'The truth will make you free,' said Jesus. But 'What is truth?' say many along with Pontius Pilate. 'I am the truth,' says Jesus, and 'if you continue in my word, you are truly my disciples, and you will know the truth.' John 8:31–2, RSV. Christian doctrine attempts to summarise and arrange in an orderly way the truth that Jesus taught and his apostles developed.

Christian faith is having a hard time in many parts of Western Europe, but across the world it is a vigorous, growing and dynamic movement. Among Christians in Britain there is widespread interest in and concern about the Bible and Christian experience, about evangelism and worship, about spirituality and ethical issues. But *doctrine* is not popular.

Doctrine seems close to being doctrinaire; dogma smacks of being dogmatic. A widespread perception is that doctrine is boring and difficult; it is irrelevant to real life, spirituality, evangelism and the great ethical problems; it is divisive and dangerous because it encourages bigotry. Some of those accusations have real point. Doctrine has generally not been well taught, either in college or church. Where it is popular it is sometimes a rigid and narrow system.

The writers of this book want to see a real change. I have invited seven other contributors who are specialists in different areas of Christian discipleship to demonstrate how important doctrine is. It is relevant and it can be interesting. Without it, Christian life and faith is in danger of being like a body without its bone structure correctly co-ordinated. No doubt the skeleton should not be too intrusive, but without it firmly behind the scene, the muscles, vital organs and flesh would be in big trouble. So with Christian life – without a good doctrinal framework, the strength of Christians, the vital activities of evangelism and ethics, and the beauty of spirituality and worship will not survive in a healthy way.

We pray that God's truth will be known, loved, lived and shared – to the glory of God, and for the well-being of his people and world.

*   *   *

The initial vision and outline of the book emerged from the Theology Group of the Church of England Evangelical Council which the editor chaired.

Gordon Kuhrt

1

Why Doctrine?
The Confession of a
Disillusioned Liberal

Alister McGrath

Doctrine! The very word sends shivers down a lot of spines these days. Doesn't an interest in doctrine make you a doctrinaire person – the sort of petty and pedantic person whom the modern church could very well do without? It conjures up images of fussy theologians, closeted in their studies and isolated from the real world, scrabbling furiously and pointlessly over words. Doctrine seems like a relic of a bygone age. It may have been important once upon a time. But not now. It is an irrelevance to modern Christian faith and Christian life.

I used to think like that. I don't any more, and would like to explain why not. Maybe the way my own thinking changed will be of use to other people, as they think through much the same questions today. My conviction that doctrine is of vital importance to the mission, ministry and spirituality of the church arose through several years sustained wrestling with the question of the relevance of doctrine. It is a conviction I adopted, not one I inherited.

My own background is that of someone who became

a Christian as a student at Oxford University, through the Oxford Inter-Collegiate Christian Union. I came up to Oxford well versed in Marxism. I had been especially committed to the writings of Theodore Adorno, and had chosen to study at Wadham College on account of its historical associations with Marx and its continued association with left-wing causes. But I was beginning to have my doubts about Marxism. There were just too many unanswered questions. 1971 was probably the heyday of Marxist influence at Oxford, and my doubts seemed out of place.

I began to rethink things. I had never given all that much consideration to Christianity, which I had tended to regard as little more than some form of spiritual narcotic to deaden the pain of life – quite unnecessary for someone like myself, who was perfectly capable of coping with things. I found myself reopening old questions I thought I had buried, and allowing myself to listen to ideas I had never really taken seriously. By the end of my first term, I knew that Christianity had something far more satisfactory – and far more *moral* – than Marxism to offer the world, myself included. I became a Christian, and can honestly say I have never looked back since then.

But I was determined to be a *thinking* Christian. After completing my undergraduate and research degrees in the natural sciences, I began to study theology seriously, eventually taking a degree in the subject at Oxford. At that stage, the Oxford University Faculty of Theology could fairly be said to have been dominated by a gentle liberal Protestantism. Perhaps a number of its members may have even seen their educational objectives to be to encourage students to become liberal Protestants, like themselves. Evangelicalism always seemed to be treated as something intellectually despicable, whereas liberalism was commendable. All too often, the call for students to 'think for themselves' seemed to amount to a demand that they think like their (theologically liberal!) teachers.

Christianity without doctrine

At any rate, I found that my youthful views on the nature of Christianity were often ridiculed as unworthy of serious consideration. I realised that I had become a liberal – someone who looked to human reason and secular culture, instead of scripture, for religious guidance and inspiration. I went on to train for the priesthood of the Church of England at Westcott House, Cambridge, then firmly established as the flagship of liberal catholicism within the Anglican theological colleges. My shift away from evangelicalism to liberalism seemed to be justified by events in 1977, which witnessed the publication of the essay collection *The Myth of God Incarnate* and James Barr's *Fundamentalism*[1] – works which finally persuaded me that evangelicalism totally lacked serious intellectual content, and had been totally rejected by mainstream academic life.

But I kept thinking throughout my period at Cambridge, and on into my curacy at a suburban parish in Nottingham. And I found myself plagued by doubts. It seemed increasingly to me that liberal Anglicanism often amounted to little more than a conglomerate of transient theological responses to events in the academic world. It seemed as if there was no theological or spiritual core. As I struggled with the issues thrown up by preaching and pastoral work, I found myself continually wondering whether liberalism actually had anything to say to the world, other than uncritically endorsing its latest trends.

Space does not permit me to write about these anxieties here, nor about the way in which I regained confidence in my evangelicalism. That would demand a book in its own right, and it is unlikely that anyone would be especially interested in it. But my reflections on the importance of doctrine are of relevance to the readers of this book.

The sort of ideas I had entertained during the five or so years of my liberal phase could be summarised along the following lines. Christianity is about bringing into the modern world the same breadth of spirit, the same compassion and care, the same depth of spiritual awareness, that was first shown to the world in the person of Jesus of Nazareth. Christianity is about action and attitudes, not about the cold, barren and outdated world of dogmas. We should not believe *in* Jesus, but *with* Jesus. Like many a young man, I found the romantic image of a 'Christianity without doctrine' profoundly attractive. It seemed to represent the best of all possible worlds, combining a rhetorical appeal to the great Western liberal deities of intellectual freedom and personal integrity with an unashamed, almost mystical, sentimental fascination, focused upon the distant hero-figure of Jesus himself. Here was a living person, whose gospel consisted in the simplicities of commitment and obedience. The demand to follow him was a call to imitate him in his relation to God and to others. We are called to imitate him, to copy him, to pattern ourselves upon him.

Simple solutions are attractive, yet seductive. As I reflected upon my liberal understanding of Christianity, I began to appreciate how intellectually shallow it was. 'Christianity without doctrine' seemed to me increasingly untenable. Why? Let me explain.[2]

The question of truth

The basic difficulty was that liberalism seemed to fudge the question of truth. This concern came home to me as I wrestled with the pastoral relevance of the incarnation. To many of my colleagues in the ministry, the incarnation was simply a symbol of God's commitment to the whole created order. I was told that it was relevant (where much doctrine was not), in that it gave theological justification to ministry, encouraging us to affirm the creation, and get involved with it.

And I have no doubt that the incarnation is of relevance and importance in these contexts. But another question seemed relevant to me: Is it true? And if it was true, was this all that there was to it? If Jesus really was God, surely it had greater and more astonishing implications than the affirmation of pastoral ministry!

This point came home to me increasingly persistently, as I tried to console the bereaved in my parish ministry. The funeral liturgy resonates with the hope of resurrection, grounded securely in the resurrection of Jesus Christ. My liberal colleagues didn't seem to find this a problem. 'It's just a symbol of hope,' they told me. 'It helps people cope with death.' It didn't matter whether it was 'true'; what mattered was whether it was 'helpful' (like believing in tooth fairies or Santa Claus). Beneath all the rhetoric about relevance lay a profoundly disturbing possibility: that people might base their lives upon an illusion, upon a blatant lie – whether the resurrection, or the incarnation. As any historian knows, the attractiveness of a belief is all too often inversely proportional to its truth.

An example will make my point clearer. In the sixteenth century, the radical writer and preacher Thomas Müntzer led a revolt of German peasants against their political masters. On the morning of the decisive encounter between the peasants and the armies of the German princes, Müntzer promised that those who followed him would be unscathed by the weapons of their enemies. Encouraged by this attractive and meaningful belief, the peasants stiffened their resolve. The outcome was a catastrophe. Six thousand peasants were slaughtered in the ensuing battle, and six hundred captured. Barely a handful escaped. Their belief in invulnerability was relevant. It was attractive. It was meaningful. It was also a crude and cruel lie, without any foundation in truth. The last hours of that pathetic group of trusting men rested on an utter illusion. It was only when the first salvoes cut some of their number to ribbons that they realised that they had been deceived.

To allow 'relevance' to be given greater weight than truth seemed to me to be a mark of intellectual shallowness and moral irresponsibility. The first, and most fundamental, of all questions must be: Is it true? Is this worthy of belief and trust? Once this has been established, the relevance of the belief in question may be considered. Truth is certainly no guarantee of relevance – but no one can build their personal life around a lie. And thus I came to see the importance of doctrine. It aims to tell the truth about things. What you do with that truth – morally, spiritually or pastorally – is secondary to establishing that truth in the first place.

The way things are

Christian doctrine aims to describe the ways things are. It is concerned to tell the truth, in order that we may enter into and act upon that truth. It is an expression of a responsible and caring faith – a faith which is prepared to give an account of itself, and to give careful consideration to its implications for the way in which we live. To care about doctrine is to care about the reliability of the foundations of the Christian life. It is to be passionately concerned that our actions and attitudes, our hopes and our fears, are a response to *God* – not something or someone making claims to divinity, which collapse upon closer inspection.

Perhaps the German church struggle of the 1930s high-lights the importance of doctrine to the modern church. When Adolf Hitler came to power, he demanded that he and the Nazi government of the Third Reich should have authority over the church and its preaching. The German church polarised into two factions: the 'German Christians', who believed the church should respond positively to National Socialism, and the 'Confessing Church' – including such writers as Karl Barth and Dietrich Bonhoeffer – who believed that the church was answerable to Jesus Christ, and him alone. Representatives of this 'Confessing Church' met at Barmen in 1934, where they issued the famous *Barmen Declaration*, perhaps one of the finest statements of the Lordship of Jesus Christ over his church and its implications:

'I am the way, and the truth and the life. No-one comes to the Father except through me.' (John 14:6)
    'I tell you the truth, the man who does not enter the

sheep pen by the gate, but climbs in some other way, is a thief and a robber . . . I am the gate; whoever enters through me will be saved.' (John 10:1, 9)

Jesus Christ, as he is revealed to us in Holy Scripture, is the one Word of God which we have to hear and which we have to trust and obey in life and in death.

We reject the false doctrine, that the church could and would have to acknowledge as a source of its proclamation or as the revelation of God any events and powers, figures and truths, other than this one Word of God.

In other words, the church cannot and must not substitute anything (for example, the state government or German culture in the 1930s; or liberal humanism in the 1990s) or anyone (such as Adolf Hitler in the 1930s; or the ideas of some cult novelist or writers in the 1990s) for Jesus Christ. If the church ever loses her faithful obedience to her Lord, she has lost her life and her soul.

Who to obey

Doctrine thus defines who we are to obey. It draws a firm line of demarcation between a false church, which answers to the pressures of the age, and a true church, which is obedient and responsible to God, as he has revealed himself in Jesus Christ. 'True knowledge of God is born out of obedience' (John Calvin).[3] Inattention to doctrine robs a church of her reason for existence, and opens the way to enslavement and oppression by the world. The German Christians, through well-intentioned but muddled attitudes towards the world, allowed that world to conquer them. The same could too easily happen to us as well.

A church which takes doctrine seriously is a church which is obedient to and responsible for what God has entrusted to it. Doctrine gives substance and weight to what the Christian church has to offer to the world. A

church which despises or neglects doctrine may simply
lapse into a comfortable conformity with the world – or
whatever part of the world it happens to feel most at home
with. Its agenda is set by the world; its presuppositions
are influenced by the world; its outlook mirrors that of
the world. There are few more pathetic sights than a
church wandering aimlessly from one 'meaningful' issue
to another in a desperate search for relevance in the eyes
of the world.

But there is more to it than this. One of my reasons
for adopting liberalism had been the pervasive perception within academic circles at Oxford and Cambridge
that thinking people could not be evangelicals (and vice
versa). Yet more and more I found that certain ways
of thinking were, in effect, ruled out in advance by
liberalism. It seemed increasingly to me that liberal values
determined liberal theology. (For example, the uniqueness
of Christ was rejected, on account of its implications for
inter-religious dialogue. This dialogue was seen to be a
good thing; therefore, any doctrines which happened to
get in its way were eliminated.[4])

A critical approach?

But where did those values come from? They seemed to
be little more than an uncritical repetition of the views of
liberal society at large. Having been attracted to liberalism
by its agenda of 'adopting a critical approach', I found that
this critical approach was only applied to certain matters
(for example, scripture), and appeared to be used rather
sparingly in other areas (such as with regard to the values
of secular liberal society, or the validity of appealing
to common human experience as a central theological
resource). This selectivity raised doubts in my mind. It
seemed that culture was allowed to criticise Christianity –
but that Christianity was not allowed to criticise culture.
In any case, the liberal agenda seemed to deprive it of the
resources it needed to do this. No doctrines; no foundation
for a criticism of society.

Who is Jesus?

This point led me on to reflect on the relevance of Jesus Christ to the Christian faith. In my liberal phase, I – like many of my colleagues – dismissed doctrines about the person of Christ as an irrelevance to life. The incarnation, to return to the example noted above, was not so much a doctrine about the person of Christ, but a symbol affirming God's involvement in the world. But gradually I found myself realising that I had to be able to give an account of who Jesus was. That question could not be postponed indefinitely. One had to spell out what it was about him that made him so central to Christianity.

So what were the options? Jesus must be more than just a religious teacher to account for his position within Christianity. C. S. Lewis expressed this point clearly and trenchantly:

> We have never followed the advice of the great teachers. Why are we likely to begin now? Why are we more likely to follow Christ than any of the others? Because he's the best moral teacher? But that makes it even less likely that we shall follow him. If Christianity only means one more bit of good advice, then Christianity is of no importance. There's been no lack of good advice over the last four thousand years. A bit more makes no difference.[5]

In fact, however, Christians do not speak of Jesus in this way, as Lewis stresses. They speak of being 'saved' through him. They speak about encountering God through him.

In any case, the teaching of Jesus himself carries us beyond the idea that Jesus is only a teacher. The outrage provoked by Jesus among his Jewish audience when he declared that the paralytic's sins were forgiven (Mark 2:5) was utterly genuine. Their theology was utterly correct: 'Who can forgive sins but God alone?' (Mark 2:7). Jesus' words point back to himself. If they are to be taken seriously, they amount to a remarkable statement concerning Jesus himself. His identity and status become part of this message. His statements about God are mingled with statements concerning himself, even to the point where the reliability and trustworthiness of the former come to depend upon the latter. The statements concerning what Jesus believes himself to be called and able to do require clarification of the relationship between Jesus and God, between the Son and the Father – and thus point to the need for doctrines, such as that of the incarnation.

To allow that Jesus is a religious teacher is to raise the question of his authority. Why should we take him seriously? We have been fortunate enough to have had the advice of countless moral and religious teachers in human history – what makes Jesus different? What singles him out as commanding attention? It is untenable to suggest that Jesus' authority rests upon the excellence of his moral or religious teaching. To make this suggestion is to imply that Jesus has authority only when he happens to agree with us. We thus would have authority over Jesus.

I did originally believe that the authority of Christ rests upon the excellence of his moral and religious teaching. This position initially sounds attractive; on closer inspection, however, it turns out actually to undermine that very authority. By what standards do we judge Jesus' teaching? The argument rests on knowing in advance what moral or religious teachings are to be regarded as outstanding. Jesus Christ is then regarded as authoritative, to the extent that he echoes these already existing standards. He is judged by a higher authority – what these writers regard as morally and religiously acceptable. For classical Christian thought, it is existing human religious and moral ideas which are to be challenged and judged by Jesus Christ; for these modern writers, it is existing notions of morality and religion which are to judge Jesus Christ. Christ is thus placed firmly under human authority, denied any role of challenging and overturning accepted human ideas and values.

It may seem very attractive to see Jesus as some sort of projection or validation of our own standards and aspirations. Yet if we allow that Jesus has authority simply because he echoes what we happen to believe to be right, we are setting ourselves above him in judgement. It is our own concepts of morality, our own standards (wherever they come from) that are judging him. And all too often those standards are little more than the prejudices of our own culture. By judging Jesus in this way, we lock ourselves into our own situation. We are prisoners of our culture, unable to see its limitations. We are unwilling to accept criticism from outside it. If Jesus echoes our own values and aspirations, we gladly accept his support; if Jesus should happen to challenge them, we dismiss him, or choose to ignore the challenge.

Jesus is thus denied any possibility of transforming us by challenging our presuppositions. We are reluctant to hear him when he does not echo our own liberal voices. (The rush to 'contextualise' or 'relativise' Jesus where he seems to conflict with modern values is an interesting illustration of this process.) If Jesus has any authority in this way, it is simply as a passive echo of our own ideas and values.

It is for this reason that doctrine is of central importance. Christianity does not assert that Christ has authority on account of the excellence or acceptability of his teaching; rather, the teaching of Christ has authority and validity on account of who he is – God incarnate. The object of Christian faith is not the teachings, but the teacher. The New Testament provides ample justification of this point; throughout his writings, Paul begins by making doctrinal affirmations, and then proceeds to draw moral conclusions. Doctrine comes first; moral and religious principles follow. For example, the doctrine of the resurrection leads to an attitude of hope in the face of adversity; the doctrine of the incarnation of Christ leads to an attitude of humility on the part of believers; the doctrine of the reconciliation of believers to God through Christ leads to a plea that believers should be reconciled with one another.

The inevitability of doctrine

In fact, the identity and significance of Jesus can only be spelled out in doctrinal terms. 'We cannot go on treating and believing in Jesus Christ in a way in which it would be wrong to treat and believe in another man, without a theory of his person that explains that he is something more than man' (Charles Gore).[6] It is doctrine which explains why and how Jesus' words and deeds have divine, rather than purely human, authority. It is doctrine which singles out Jesus Christ, and none other, as being God incarnate. Quite contrary to the Broad Church liberals of the nineteenth century (who believed it was possible to uphold the religious and ethical aspects of Christianity, while discarding its doctrines) and their spiritual heirs of today, the authority of Jesus' moral and religious teaching thus rests firmly upon a doctrinal foundation.

This point was made clearly and prophetically by William Temple. Writing against the 'Religion without Dogma' movement in 1942, he declared that:

> You would hardly find any theologian now who supposes that Christian ethics can survive for half a century in detachment from Christian doctrine, and this is the very last moment when the church itself can come forward with outlines of Christian ethics in the absence of the theological foundation which alone makes them really tenable. Our people have grown up in a generally Christian atmosphere, and take it for granted that all people who are not actually perverted hold what are essentially Christian notions about human conduct. But this is not true.[7]

(Temple then goes on to illustrate this point with reference to the rise of Hitler and Stalin in the 1930s.) Although many liberal and radical writers of the 1960s suggested that Christian ethics could be divorced from doctrine, and maintain an independent existence, the wisdom of

Temple's words is once more apparent. As recent writers such as Oliver O'Donovan have insisted, distinctive *ethics* (whether Marxist, Christian or Buddhist) are dependent upon *world-views*, which are in turn shaped by *doctrines*, by understandings of human nature and destiny.[8]

Liberalism seemed to me to teach that doctrine was superfluous. Yet I gradually realised that liberalism had its own doctrines. The economist J. M. Keynes came across similar attitudes among industrialists and politicians. 'We're practical people who have no need for abstract theories about economics,' they declared. Yet these people, Keynes scathingly remarked, were little more than the unwitting slaves of some defunct economist. Their allegedly 'practical' outlook actually rested upon unacknowledged economic theories. They lacked the insight to see that what they regarded as obvious was actually based upon the theories of some long-dead economist.

Liberalism, I realised, itself rests upon quite definite doctrinal foundations, despite allowing itself to be represented as an anti-doctrinal movement. The study of doctrine is thus profoundly liberating, as it exposes these hidden doctrinal assumptions. Every version of Christianity that has ever existed rests upon doctrinal foundations; not every version of Christianity has grasped this fact. The genuine question of importance is quite simple: Which of those doctrinal foundations are the most authentic and reliable?

How is the 'cross' good news?

This point became increasingly clear to me as I reflected on the question of why Christianity can be said to be good news. I found the importance of this question to my pastoral work becoming ever more evident during my time in the parish. Time and time again, my regular parish visiting suggested that people had real difficulty in understanding how the death of a man two thousand years ago could be good news for them today. The liberal vocabulary of the cross began to seem rather pathetic to me, as it so obviously failed to gain a hearing.

Now, it had been drilled into me that liberalism was relevant to the modern world, where evangelicalism was not. Yet liberal approaches to the cross seemed an irrelevance in my parish ministry. It is not good news if a man, after a life of self-giving and care for his fellows, should be harried, tortured, mocked and finally executed in a triumphant display of barbarity. It is no gospel if this man reveals the love of one human being for another, far far away and long long ago.

It becomes good news, however, if it is the Son of God himself who gives himself in order that we might come to newness of life. It becomes good news if these events are interpreted in terms of a sufficiently high profile of identity between Jesus and God, such as that set out by the doctrine of the incarnation. The cross is good news because it proclaims the reality of the love of God to the world. It points to Jesus Christ upon the cross, and declares, 'God loved the world this much' (see John 3:16). The death of Jesus Christ upon the cross is therefore only good news if it is interpreted in a certain way.

Doctrine defines how the cross of Christ is to be interpreted. To put it another way, it provides an interpretative framework for understanding the events of Calvary. Doctrine aims to explain what it is about the life, death and resurrection of Jesus Christ which is good news. It aims to explain and justify the vital connection between the 'there and then' of Calvary and the 'here and now' of our own situation. It is an interpretative bridge between history and faith, between the past and the present. It relates the events of Calvary to our own experience, interpreting the latter in terms of the former.

Doctrine and the mind

Doctrine also represents a natural outcome of human inquisitiveness and intelligence. Human beings are rational creatures. They ask questions – questions like: 'Why?' As

Plato stressed, there is a natural human desire to 'give an account of things'. Why are we being asked to accept the teachings of Jesus Christ? Why is he singled out among other human beings? This need to make sense of things applies equally to matters of Christian faith. For example, the crucifixion and resurrection are things which need to be explained. Why did they happen? What do they mean? In his 1891 Bampton Lectures, delivered at Oxford University, Charles Gore pointed out that this natural human inquisitiveness has its religious outcome in doctrine:

> Christians found themselves treating Jesus Christ, believing in Jesus Christ, as they had never treated or believed in any other man . . . Because they were rational they must have asked themselves 'Why do we treat Jesus Christ in this exceptional manner? Who is he to be so treated? What is his relation to God whose functions he exercises? Why are we not idolaters if we yield him such worship?' They must have asked these questions because they were men endowed with reason, and could not therefore go on acting without giving some account of their action.[9]

Doctrine is nothing other than the attempt of rational believers to make sense of every aspect of their experience of Jesus Christ. If conversion involves the mind as well as the soul, doctrine is its inevitable outcome, as the believer brings his or her mind to bear on the implications of faith. To be a *thinking* Christian is to be aware of the need for, and importance of, doctrine.

Doctrine thus attempts to make explicit the implicit assumptions of faith. For example, faith believes that we have been saved through Jesus Christ; doctrine asserts that this belief implies that Jesus must be both God and man if this is to be possible. Doctrine is basically the outcome of taking rational trouble over the mysteries of faith. To prohibit this rational reflection in order to develop a 'Christianity without doctrine' is to deny Christians the right to think about their faith. Doctrinal reflection is the product of a passionate search for truth, combining intellectual curiosity and honesty.

To be concerned about doctrine is not to be obsessed with petty matters; it is to be aware of the enormous responsibility placed upon us, as we try to grasp exactly what God is like, and what that might entail for our hearts and minds. *Doctrine* matters because *God* matters – and because we matter to God. If God has taken so much trouble to enter into our pathetic and sinful world, the very least we can do is to be attentive to him. Doctrine is the outcome of a caring and committed attentiveness on our part to God telling us about himself.

Only a fool would imagine that doctrine pretends to state exhaustively everything about God in the form of human words. But words are the only means at our disposal to tell others about God, and about his nature and purposes. That means we must get those words right. It means taking care to use words responsibly. Doctrine aims to assist our talk about God, guiding us as we try to explain the gospel to outsiders, or gain a deeper understanding of it ourselves, or think through its implications for our society. To those who mutter darkly about doctrine getting in the way of the real business of life, it may be said that doctrine does not preclude, but informs, action. It forces us to think through what sort of action is most in line with the patterns God himself has set us, in the person of Jesus Christ and in the testimony of scripture. As church history makes painfully clear, not all the actions of the church merit the name 'Christian'. Doctrine aims to ensure that *our* actions do.

There is far more to Christianity than doctrine. The Puritan slogan 'truth in life' has much to commend it. Doctrine affects life. It determines values, and thus actions. It is like the bones which give strength and shape to the human body. It is like the steel rods which reinforce concrete structures. Without doctrine, faith becomes shapeless, weak and vulnerable. Doctrine addresses, interprets and transforms human experience, in order that a dynamic, living and resilient faith may result. Doctrine inside the head is an irrelevance; life without doctrine is an impossibility.

Doctrine and life complement each other – and are *meant* to complement each other. The doctrine of a loving God who became incarnate in his world gives rise to loving people, who aim to serve God in that same world. The doctrine of the forgiveness of our sins gives birth to a forgiving people, just as the doctrine of the resurrection of the dead brings into being a people of hope, who know their final destiny lies outside this world. Doctrine enables God's story to express itself in our story, and transform it. George Herbert's little-known poem 'The Windows' brings out this point rather well:

> Lord, how can man preach thy eternall word?
>   He is a brittle crazie glasse:
> Yet in thy temple thou dost him afford
>   This glorious and transcendent place,
>   To be a window, through thy grace.
>
> But when thou dost anneal in glasse thy storie,
>   Making thy life to shine within
> The holy Preachers; then the light and glorie
>   More rev'rend grows, and more doth win:
>   Which else shows watrish, bleak, and thin.
>
> Doctrine and life, colours and light, in one
>   When they combine and mingle, bring,
> A strong regard and aw: but speech alone
>   Doth vanish like a flaring thing,
>   And in the eare, not conscience ring.

Why doctrine? Because Christians think and act. That thinking and acting needs to be informed. Christianity is just too important to allow itself to be reduced to a 'watery, bleak and thin' set of ideas, or the shallowness and mindlessness of unthinking action in the world. The rest of the essays in this volume aim to spell out how doctrine affects life. The purpose of this essay is to insist that doctrine provides a firm foundation upon which the Christian life may be built. And in a world plagued by superficiality, a firm foundation remains of essential importance.

Questions for discussion

1. Can anyone be a Christian without believing *something*?
2. What are some of the uses of doctrine?
3. Why do some people find the idea of 'doctrine' very intimidating?
4. What would be the effect of eliminating doctrine from Christianity?

For further reading

James Atkinson and Rowan Williams, 'On Doing Theology', in C. Baxter (ed.), *Stepping Stones* (London: Hodder & Stoughton, 1987), 1–20

Paul Avis, *Ecumenical Theology and the Elusiveness of Doctrine* (London: SPCK, 1986)

Hendrikus Berkhof, *Christian Faith: An Introduction to the Study of the Faith* (Grand Rapids: Eerdmans, 1979)

Charles Gore, *The Incarnation of the Son of God* (London: John Murray, 1922)

Alister E. McGrath, *Understanding Doctrine* (London: Hodder & Stoughton, 1991)

Dorothy L. Sayers, 'Creed or Chaos?', in *Creed or Chaos?* (London: Methuen, 1947), pp. 25–46

Revd Dr Alister E. McGrath studied natural sciences and theology at Oxford and Cambridge. After serving as curate at St Leonard's, Wollaton, Nottingham, he took up his present position as lecturer in historical and systematic theology at Wycliffe Hall, and a member of the Oxford University Faculty of Theology. He recently delivered the Bampton Lectures at Oxford University, and the Anderson Lectures at McGill University, Montreal, and is the author of many books, both scholarly and popular.

2

Doctrine and the Bible

Donald Allister

Living apart: a sad state of affairs

The Bible is important, relevant, alive, and worth spending time on; doctrine is unimportant, irrelevant, dead, and worth avoiding: that's how many Christians think or feel. In recent years there has been a return to the Bible right across the churches, but not a return to doctrine. The Bible is seen as having something to say; doctrine is not.

Given the way that doctrine has often been presented, such an attitude is hardly surprising. It is normal for books on doctrine to be full of long words and difficult concepts which don't seem to come from scripture or to have any practical use. Doctrine has become the preserve of academics. It is something that those training for the ministry have to study, but it doesn't seem to help them with their Bible study or make them better ministers.

I believe that doctrine does matter; it is important, relevant, alive, and worth spending time on. And in the same breath I want to say that doctrine and the Bible belong together in the life and mission of the church. Neither should exist without the other, and if either doctrine or the Bible is taken on its own there will be problems. In fact, it is because doctrine and the Bible have been divorced (or at least separated) that we have so many problems in seeing the relevance of doctrine and in understanding what the Bible has to say.

Doctrine is an essential tool, given by God, to help us read, understand, explain, proclaim and obey the Bible. Without it we can do none of those things properly. Without it the Bible becomes just a collection of inspired stories and sayings, instead of being a unified and integrated whole, one book, the word of God.

That's why doctrine is important, and why I'm excited about it. That's why I want to see a healthy marriage between doctrine and the Bible. As long as the separation continues the children (that is churches, Christians, and all they are meant to be and do) will continue to suffer harm. Most will gravitate to one parent, some to the other, and all will lose out.

But isn't this a big claim for man-made doctrine, setting it alongside God's word as an equal, or at least a partner? And isn't it running the Bible down, to say that God's word needs human doctrine to explain it to us? Am I not really denying a great Reformation principle, that scripture alone contains all we need for salvation? Those are important questions. I hope that by the end of this chapter you'll be convinced that what I'm arguing for is biblical and right.

So how does this marriage of the Bible and doctrine work out? How does their partnership help the people of God and advance the kingdom?

The Bible was written over a period of at least a thousand years, by several dozen human authors. God was behind it all, and all of it is his word, but equally each part of it was written in a different style and for different reasons. God, his word, and his opinions don't change; but equally, each part of the Bible was written to a different group of people, a different human situation, a different set of problems.

Christian doctrine is the human work of systematising, putting into order, the teachings of the Bible. The Bible is like the open countryside, full of many lovely wild flowers, shrubs, grasses, different terrains and habitats. Doctrine is like a cultivated garden, where many terrains, habitats and plants have been organised by people. Nobody denies that the countryside is 'the real thing'; but neither does anyone deny that a well-planned garden helps the appreciation, enjoyment, study, growth and sometimes even the survival, of plant and animal life. A good garden is not a betrayal of the countryside, or a substitute for it, but its servant, friend and partner. That is how doctrine relates to the Bible.

Of course the wild countryside existed long before man-made gardens (at least in our fallen world), and the countryside doesn't need gardens; but in a fallen world we need gardens to appreciate the countryside. Similarly, the Bible doesn't need doctrine; but we need it if we are to get out of the Bible all that it has for us.

Three in one: doctrine to the rescue

It's time for an example of the way that doctrine helps us understand God's word. I'll take one of the most misunderstood and off-putting areas of doctrine, but also one of the most important: the doctrine of the Trinity.

Many Christians keep Trinity Sunday and have a suspicion that it is important, but they'd run a mile if asked to explain the doctrine of the Trinity. Many are happy to sing hymns or choruses with a strongly trinitarian structure and approach to God, but would never try to defend the doctrine – or even the need for a doctrine – of the Trinity. The problem is compounded by the fact that trinitarian doctrine is tied up with theological controversies dating back fifteen or sixteen hundred years.

Right through the Bible, God is spoken of in many different ways. At the beginning we are told that he created, that his Spirit brooded (or was hovering) over the waters, and that he spoke. Elsewhere in the Old Testament we find occasions when he speaks, is seen, appears (sometimes in human form), is described as having feelings, hands and feet, a voice and a back – but also as being unknowable, unapproachable, as not having a body and as not to be turned into images. He is a father, but like a mother; a friend, but an enemy; like us, but wholly different from us; our maker, lawgiver, judge and destroyer, but also our teacher, guide, helper and saviour. The list could go on: it's awe-inspiring, but confusing.

The New Testament offers more of the same. God is a consuming fire, a terrible judge, a fearful enemy, totally alien. But he's also one who loves us, cares for us, became a man and died for us, offers us himself, his friendship, his forgiveness and his strength. It's hardly surprising that books about God can be heavy, difficult and daunting. It's hardly surprising that Christian attempts to explain and proclaim what God is like have sometimes been more confusing than helpful.

But there are in the Bible clear lines of teaching about God, portrayals of him which seem to run right through or to recur regularly. In the Old Testament God is unknowable, but he makes himself known. He is our creator, not one of us, but somehow he gets alongside his people and among them. His presence is a great danger, but is also a great comfort. He is, at one and the same time, creator, redeemer and sustainer. In the New Testament Jesus both reveals God and is God. God is Spirit and cannot be seen, but is seen in Jesus. God's Spirit, and the Spirit of Jesus, and Jesus Christ, and the Spirit of Christ, and the Father, and God himself, all seem to be one and the same, yet to be doing and saying different things. Jesus is God, and a man, and the Son of God. The Spirit comes from the Father, but also from Jesus. In Jesus the whole fullness of God dwells. The Spirit brings with him into our lives both Jesus and also the Father.

The Bible's picture of God is tremendously helpful, a great source of wonder, joy and hope. But it's too much for us to cope with. We need to arrange the material, put it under various headings, clarify and simplify a stunningly complex pattern of truth, if we are to have any hope of understanding or explaining it.

In the same way as the scientist draws a simple picture of atoms and molecules as little balls joined together by sticks, knowing that the picture is true, helpful, and necessary, but also over-simplified and potentially misleading, so the theologian or preacher puts truths about God into diagrammatic form, alliterative headings, anthropomorphic language, philosophical concepts – all of which can be true, helpful and necessary, but also over-simplified and potentially misleading.

How does the biblical picture of God get turned into the doctrine of the Trinity? Doctrine is the systematisation of the Bible; that is, Bible texts and truths are put together in such a way that as clear a picture as possible emerges. If we start to do this with the different ways God is described, we might come up with something like this.

Clear texts tell us that God is the Lord God (Exod. 20:2–3), that Jesus is the Lord God (Isa. 9:6; John 20:28), and that the Holy Spirit is the Lord God (Acts 5:3–4). We're also taught that the Father and Jesus are distinct but one (John 14:9–10), that Jesus and the Spirit are distinct but one (Rom. 8:9–10), and that God and the Spirit are distinct but one (Heb. 9:14). And all three are mentioned together in various places, including Matthew 3:16–17; 28:19–20; John 14:15–20; 2 Corinthians 13:14; Hebrews 9:14; and 1 Peter 1:2.

Collecting Bible truths together like that is a large part of the job of doing doctrine! What is needed next is to produce clear statements which do justice to the texts we are considering. In fact we've already started with the statements above, such as 'Jesus and the Spirit are distinct but one'. It's then necessary to check these basic doctrinal statements against other parts of scripture. If we've got them wrong, we'll find texts or passages to contradict them. If we're right, we may well find that other previously confusing texts make more sense in the light of our doctrine.

You may think this is similar to the way some sermons are constructed. So it is. One of the techniques of the preacher is to present Bible truths under clear and memorable headings. The three 'distinct but one' statements above could well be headings for three points in a sermon on the Trinity. Good preaching is doctrinal, whatever else it is.

The doctrine of the Trinity says that there is one indivisible God. That's an important and precious Bible truth. But the doctrine also explains that God exists and acts as three persons: God the Father, God the Son, and God the Holy Spirit. Each of these is fully God, not just a part of God. Each of them is and displays what God is. But the three are distinct in their dealings with one another and with us. In other words, there is in God himself, in his one undivided perfection, a trinity of persons, wholly in tune with one another, co-operating not competing, distinct not disagreeing, separate not pulling apart. God is one and three, three-in-one and one-in-three. This is not a case of double schizophrenia, but a sort of existence we do not see elsewhere: unity and community, oneness and multiplicity, singular and plural.

To quote the Athanasian Creed, one of the very ancient statements of belief agreed by leaders of all the churches in about AD 400:

> We worship one God in Trinity, and Trinity in Unity; neither confounding [confusing] the persons nor dividing the substance. For there is one person of the Father, another of the Son and another of the Holy Ghost. But the Godhead of the Father, and of the Son, and of the Holy Ghost is all one: the Glory equal, the Majesty co-eternal.

That is pure doctrine, expressing Bible truths as clear definitions. Obviously it's old, and some of the language is a bit technical ('persons' and 'substance' in particular), but it does the job very effectively once we understand the meaning of the words.

The doctrine of the Trinity is the best, most helpful, most accurate attempt so far to explain the nature of God and the interrelationship of God, Jesus and the Holy Spirit. As we have it, it is the culmination of hundreds of years of thinking, praying, talking and arguing by believers. It is not simple, but it is simpler than the Bible. It is a tool to help us understand the Bible. It is a gift of God to his church. Without it we would have more difficulty than we do in understanding or explaining how God, Jesus and the Holy Spirit relate to each other and to us.

Theory and practice

One objection to doctrine is that it is always theory with no practice. Theoretical doctrine is important, but so is the practical. Very often we think of doctrine as just theory, and that makes it seem irrelevant (interesting perhaps, but of no real use). In fact every 'theoretical' doctrine has a clear practical side and implications, and when doctrine is well taught these will come over loud and clear. The doctrine of the Trinity is no exception to this.

The doctrine of the Trinity is not just theory, saying what God is like. It also tells us how he works, and particularly how he works for us in salvation. The practical doctrine tells of: the Father's love for us and his plan of salvation; the Son's work on the cross for us, reconciling us to the Father; and the Spirit's work in the hearts of believers, applying the benefits won by Christ, making Christ known, and assuring us of the Father's love. These statements are summaries and headings, representing many different Bible passages; but when put together they form practical doctrine.

A doctrinal statement of the Trinity at work in salvation, such as in the last paragraph, is an enormous help to believers reflecting on their relationship with God; but it is also invaluable to those doing evangelism. Explaining in clear language what God has done and how he works is one of the major tasks of the evangelist. The theologian, producing that language, is serving evangelism, making it easier for the evangelist to preach and for the hearer to understand. Doctrine is very practical.

Preaching and teaching

One of the main reasons why doctrine arose, and why we need it, is to help preachers and teachers explain Christian truth. If you read the first few verses of Genesis, you get a picture of God in creation, but it is a bit vague and even confusing. If you read in the light of the biblical doctrine of the Trinity, you begin to see more of what's going on: the creator is the triune God. This helps us to understand New Testament statements that Jesus Christ was involved in creation (e.g., John 1:3; Col. 1:16). The doctrine, drawn from the whole Bible, helps us to understand those parts of scripture which are less clear.

Sometimes this is described as reading the Bible through doctrinal spectacles, and people criticise it because they say it is not letting the Bible itself speak, but coming to it with our presuppositions or prejudices. That needs to be answered, because it certainly is possible to bring our prejudices to Bible reading.

In the first place, this method is letting the Bible speak for itself, because the doctrine is the Bible speaking. What is really going on is that the Bible, using doctrine as a tool, is explaining itself. Or, to put it the other way round, we are looking at one part of the Bible in the light of the whole. This is perfectly reasonable, and indeed is a good methodology, given the belief that the whole Bible was inspired by the one consistent Spirit of God.

Second, we guard against the danger of bringing prejudice to our doctrinal Bible reading by continually checking our doctrine against the teaching of scripture. If, on the basis of a few texts, I make a doctrinal statement which helps me explain another harder text, that is fine. But if the doctrinal statement is contradicted by a text elsewhere, then I know I've got it wrong. The doctrine needs to be rewritten to include all the relevant biblical teaching. Preachers and teachers have a clear duty to make sure that their words agree with the whole of the Bible, not just parts of it.

This means that doctrinal statements are always provisional: we must be ready to improve or correct them as we come across or understand Bible passages that we haven't fully taken into account in constructing the doctrine. Doctrine is thus more like a loose-leaf notebook than a bound volume. That doesn't mean it is of little value; the classical doctrine of the Trinity, formulated fifteen hundred years ago, has stood the test of time and has yet to be bettered. That is true of most of the doctrinal statements stemming from the sixteenth-century Reformation, including the theologies of Luther, and Calvin, and the great statements of faith of the Anglican, Baptist, and Presbyterian churches. We must be ready to revise our doctrine, but only when we see that it does not match up to scripture.

Countering heresy

Another reason why doctrine developed, and we need it today, was to counter heresy. I'm a firm believer in the old saying that the greatest danger to the church is always from within, not from outside; and that heresy is the greatest danger of all. Jesus was so insistent on God's word and his words being the truth ('amen' or 'verily' means 'truly'), and he calls the Holy Spirit 'the Spirit of truth'.

A basic heresy, actually the cause of many others, is that there are inconsistencies or disagreements within the Bible. For example, we often hear that the Old Testament presents one idea of God and the New Testament another, or that Paul's doctrine is much more rigid than that of Jesus. These views only arise because people see the Bible as lots of little bits rather than a coherent whole. Because true doctrine always attempts to systematise scripture, it will constantly argue against, and disprove, the notion of biblical contradictions. The idea that the Bible is one book, the product of one mind (as well as of many), and consistent throughout, is what lies behind all genuine Christian doctrine, and deals the death-blow to virtually all heresy.

One of the most dangerous heresies in the early church (and today) was that Jesus was just a good man, even a Spirit-filled man, but not actually God. A similar one was the more subtle but equally wrong idea that he was born human but became divine later on (at his baptism in some versions of the heresy, and at the resurrection in others). The effect of these views is to deny the incarnation and thus to say that we humans (in the person of Jesus) reach up to share in the life of God. The correct view is that in Jesus God was reaching down to us, that in the incarnation Jesus took on our humanity, became fully man, while remaining fully God.

Behind that correct view lies the biblical doctrine of the Trinity. People deny Jesus' divinity because they don't understand or don't believe the doctrine of the Trinity. If they did, they would know that the second person of the Trinity, the Son of God, who existed before creation, is the one who took human form and became known as Jesus of Nazareth. This truth explains some of Jesus' own sayings about himself, and makes sense of things written about him in scripture.

The doctrine developed because of wrong views, and if the doctrine is properly taught today, such wrong views will be less likely to gain ground. The battle against heresy, especially heresy arising within the church, is as real as it ever was. Christians, particularly ministers and preachers, are called by God to stand firm in the true faith and to guard or defend it. That guarding has a strong positive aspect: in part, we guard the gospel by proclaiming it. But it also has its important negative side: we guard the truth by refuting error. Doctrine is an essential tool in refuting error, and if doctrine is neglected we are in danger of going astray from the Bible's teaching.

Doctrine apart from the Bible

Another danger is that doctrine will lose its essential linkage with scripture. This has happened in the world of academic theology to an alarming degree, and much of the havoc wrought there has worked its way into churches. So-called doctrine with no apparent connection to the Bible creates all sorts of problems. It introduces wrong thinking and heresy. It becomes simply an academic exercise and so puts off those Christians who are less academic. It harms the cause of real biblical doctrine by making people think that doctrine is an optional extra and not of central importance. Doctrine must stem from Bible study, it must be seen as the servant of the Bible, and it must constantly be reassessed in the light of continuing Bible study.

There is a further danger when attitudes to doctrine and ways of doing it go wrong. This is that doctrine can easily be taken over by the world or by worldly ways of thinking. Again, this has happened in much modern theology. The activity of doing theology, making doctrine, is often not seen as explaining or systematising the Bible, but as trying to make sense of the world in the light of what we know or feel or guess about God. This means that the all-important headings used in doctrine are chosen not to explain scripture but to be relevant to theologians' ideas of what is really important. The result is that many modern theologians are really writing sociology or anthropology, politics or economics. Those are genuine academic disciplines, but they aren't the same as Christian doctrine.

It is within the church, the believing community, that the task of developing and reshaping doctrine must be done. Part of the reason for the rampant liberalism we see today, where theologians virtually ignore the Bible or feel free to disagree with it, is that people try to do their theology outside the church. They operate within universities and colleges, creating an academic so-called theology which is of no use at all for the believer wanting to understand the Bible better. Or they root themselves in the world, claiming to be relevant but in fact compromising the authority of the Bible. The church is the only place to do theology properly.

The church is the place where the battles most need to

be fought. Traditions quickly ossify; the vital breath of scripture, interpreted and applied by doctrine, is the only way to prevent that or cure it. Some traditions are good, some may even be necessary as part of our faithfulness to God, but all tradition must be regularly tested and reviewed in the light of scripture: this is a major part of the purpose of doctrine.

The doctrine of the Trinity is an example of doctrine controlled by the Bible. The doctrine arose because of the need to understand and explain what scripture teaches on a theme which is important to scripture. It's not just that people found a few verses on an obscure topic and turned them into a major doctrine. The Bible itself was allowed to say what was important – in this case what God in himself is like – and then to develop that theme.

This contrasts sharply with some modern so-called doctrine, where people decide what is important, then try to develop a doctrine of it. If the Bible has something to say, that will be taken into account; if not, Christians can still think and discuss and come up with a 'doctrine'. So today we have these modern types of doctrine covering such subjects as nuclear weapons and political liberation, animal rights and world development. Those are subjects on which Christians should develop a view. Christian involvement in such things is important, not least because it will balance some of the wilder ideas. But they are not the subjects of theology or doctrine. They are very valid areas for Christian reflection and debate: but doctrine is something more than Christian reflection – it is Christian truth.

The shape of doctrine, the context in which it is done, the headings and subheadings, the structure, categories and language, must all be controlled by scripture. The Bible must set the agenda for doctrine. Otherwise we are in the nonsense world of some modern theologians, for whom theology is simply reflecting on any event or experience in the light of their faith (often a faith in which scripture is not very important). True theology will reflect on what is going on, but always in the light

of the Bible and in such a way that the Bible is in
control.

The blood of the lamb: doctrine in history

I want to move away from the doctrine of the Trinity to
another important area which shows something of how
doctrine should continue to develop (under the control of
the Bible): the question of the atonement, how Christ's
death achieves our reconciliation with God. It's a theme
that runs right through the Bible, especially when we make
the vital connection between Jesus as the Lamb of God and
the Old Testament sacrificial lambs. And it's an area of
doctrine whose development in history was much slower
than the Trinity, so we can see some of the stages more
clearly.

A word of warning: we now see the Bible in the light
of two thousand years of Christian doctrine. Biblical
phrases like 'justification by faith' are full of meaning
for many because of the Reformation (or the current
Anglican–Roman Catholic dialogue). But in this section
we're going back in time to when such phrases existed but
weren't understood or seen as particularly important. You
may therefore already be familiar with the endpoint of this
journey: don't let that blind you to the instructive sights
along the way.

The way atonement works is not simple. There are
many sides to it in the Bible, and many views have been
expressed over the centuries. But if we look at the history
of this doctrine we can see clear developments. Some of
them are good, adding to our understanding of scripture
and helping the church in evangelism. Others are not good,
distorting the Bible and making the church's task harder.
We'll look at a few of the main ideas.

In the early centuries after the ministry of Jesus the main
emphasis was on the crucifixion in its relation to the devil.
Some emphasised it as a victory over Satan, in that death
(his tool) was defeated. Others saw it as a ransom, paying
him his dues, so that his hostages could be set free. There

are Bible passages and verses to back up these ideas. But
it's clear (at least with our advantage of hindsight) that
there's much more to it than that.

The Middle Ages saw some important developments.
Anselm of Canterbury was born in Italy and spent most
of his life as a monk in Normandy. In 1093, at the age
of sixty, he became Archbishop of Canterbury until his
death in 1109. Anselm taught that Jesus, in his death on
the cross, was paying damages to God for human sin,
making amends by a perfect life and obedient death.
There are some problems with that view, but it was a
big step forward.

Peter Abelard (1079–1142) was a larger-than-life, never
wholly orthodox character, sometimes venerated as the
first modern free-thinker. He made a contribution to the
doctrine of the atonement by arguing that Christ's death
was effective by its moral influence on human beings. This
idea is very popular even today, lying behind theories
of Jesus as our example. Again that's a biblical idea,
but Abelard's views, while contributing to the doctrine,
are incomplete and wrong on their own. Jesus is an
example to us, but that doesn't explain why his death
was necessary: in fact, it leaves his death as a tragedy
rather than a victory, or the act of a cruel God rather
than a loving one.

The sixteenth-century Reformation saw the fullest development (so far) of the doctrine of the atonement, with the
teaching in Germany, Switzerland, England and Scotland
of penal substitution. This means that Christ died in our
place (as the Lamb of God), bearing the penalty we
deserve for our sins. Expressed this way, it both defeats
the devil (by giving death its prey, then removing its
power), and also reveals God's love (in sending his Son
to die for us).

This doctrine of penal substitution is at the heart of evangelical theology, and provides the key to most of history's
great evangelism. John Wesley and George Whitefield,
Charles Simeon, William Carey, Henry Martyn, Charles
Spurgeon, Hudson Taylor, Billy Graham: for all of them,

penal substitutionary atonement was the core of their preaching.

Theologians sometimes tried to have substitution but without the penal aspect, or to have penal but not substitutionary atonement. Others taught that we can obtain forgiveness simply by confession and turning away from sin, with no need for a blood sacrifice. Some say that Christ in his death repented on our behalf, others that Christ's death enables us to repent. All of these views, and others, end up contradicting or failing to take note of key passages in scripture.

So far, the best doctrine we have of the atonement is that of penal substitution. I've only outlined it; there is much more detail to be seen. Within this doctrine great Bible words like propitiation, righteousness and reconciliation fit into place and make a great deal of sense. It is not a popular doctrine with many people, especially those modern theologians who don't see the Bible as wholly trustworthy, or who prefer their own theories to God's revealed word; but it presents the Bible's teaching, helps us to understand some difficult Bible ideas, and serves the church in evangelism. I'm not saying it can never be bettered, just that it hasn't been yet. Until it is, by an addition or amendment that can be seen to make it more biblical, we will do well to believe it and proclaim it.

Together again: summary and conclusions

Doctrine and the Bible belong together. A good example of this is the way that doctrine should guide our preaching. In the Church of England's Book of Common Prayer, which is basically a product of the sixteenth-century Reformation, the structure of the Holy Communion service makes a very important point. The Bible readings are followed by the creed, and then the sermon. This demonstrates the way preaching should work: scripture comes first; in the creed we have doctrine which is based on scripture and must guide our approach to scripture; finally we hear the sermon, which should expound scripture in the light of biblical doctrine.

Preaching should be biblical and doctrinal. That doesn't mean it should be theory with no practical content, because doctrine (like the Bible) should be intensely practical. In fact, if either a doctrinal study or a sermon isn't applied to real life, it isn't complete. If true doctrine is a systematisation of the Bible, then its structure and headings will be every bit as practical as is the Bible itself. And the same should be true of preaching, which must be based on scripture in the light of biblical doctrine.

Doctrine is like a pair of spectacles through which to see scripture, but it is subject to, and does not control, scripture. If we look at the Bible through an unbiblical doctrinal lens, we will inevitably see it in a distorted way. If we try to look at the Bible in an impartial or 'presuppositionless' way, we are attempting the impossible. We all have our own presuppositions which influence the way we react to and understand what we read or hear. Some presuppositions are inevitable because of our background, some are valid and helpful, some are false and will lead us astray. If we want to read the Bible biblically, we must ensure that our minds and so our presuppositions are reshaped by biblical doctrine. This is what Paul means when he urges Christians to 'be transformed by the renewing of your mind' (Rom. 12:2).

This sort of doctrinal understanding is necessary to keep our thinking and teaching balanced. Without it we are likely to over-emphasise some biblical truths at the expense of other equally important ideas. It is very important to keep the right balance between, for example, law and gospel, works and faith, knowledge and experience.

It is worth looking at a few of the many examples in the Bible itself of how doctrine is used in this way. In Matthew 22:29 Jesus tells the Sadducees, 'You are in error because you do not know the Scriptures or the power of God.' In one sense they did know the scriptures, that is the content of our Old Testament. What they did not know was the

Bible's teaching on a particular topic, resurrection and life after death. It was their Bible doctrine they were weak on. In Romans 4 and Galatians 3–4 Paul applies his doctrinal understanding of Old Testament passages about Abraham, the covenant and circumcision to the New Testament church. In James 2:5 we see a doctrinal principle, drawn from many Bible verses: 'Has not God chosen those who are poor in the eyes of the world to be rich in faith and to inherit the kingdom he promised those who love him?' This then becomes the heart of James's argument against favouritism.

Doctrine is necessary to help us keep our thinking clear. So much Christian teaching and writing is woolly and vague. Those are the last words you could use to describe the ministry of Jesus or Paul, but we can all easily think of clergy and lay Christians for whom they are the first descriptions to come to mind. Clarity is important in witness, in worship, in counselling, in decision-making – in every area of Christian life and ministry. Clarity brings honour to Christ, whereas woolliness dishonours him and his word.

Doctrine will help us evaluate new insights. The Christian church doesn't yet know everything God wants to teach. He reveals his truth progressively, as we saw with the doctrine of the atonement. We would be very foolish to say that the way we understand doctrine now is going to be valid and complete for all time. Scripture is complete; nothing can be added to it; in that sense God has spoken and his revelation is complete. But our understanding of it is far from complete, and that is what doctrine is all about. We need doctrine to help us test ideas or truths which people claim to have found from scripture (or from anywhere else). If those new ideas are biblical, then our doctrine must be flexible enough to incorporate them and even be reshaped by them. If they are not (and a clear biblical doctrine will often show up their faults), we need the arguments from scripture and history which doctrine provides in order to refute them. We humans, including Christians, are as good as ever at perverting God's truth. We therefore need something, namely Christian doctrine, to protect us from ourselves.

Doctrine will help our evangelism, providing a clear framework of the gospel and clear answers to questions people ask. The best simple gospel outlines (A B C D headings, 1 2 3 lists, bridge diagrams, 'God's plan of salvation', 'Two Ways to Live', and so on) are all applied doctrine. The best manuals for counsellors at evangelistic meetings are pure doctrine, usually with suitable Bible texts included. Those who know how to answer the questions people raise are those with a good grasp of doctrine.

I end by repeating something I wrote earlier in this chapter (I'm a preacher and know that careful repetition is important in good preaching!): doctrine is an essential tool, given by God, to help us read, understand, explain, proclaim and obey the Bible. Without it we can do none of those things properly. By it we are not to distort God's word (2 Cor. 4:2), but on the contrary to handle correctly the word of truth (2 Tim. 2:15).

Questions for discussion

1. What should we do when we find a Bible text and a doctrinal statement apparently in conflict?
2. What should we do when we find two Bible texts apparently in conflict?
3. How can we test claims that God is saying something new?
4. How can we give doctrine a higher profile in our churches?
5. How can or should doctrine help us in these areas: worship, preaching, evangelism, pastoral care, social concern?

For further reading

Sinclair Ferguson and David Wright (eds.), *New Dictionary of Theology* (Leicester: Inter-Varsity Press, 1988).
A major reference book of theologians, doctrines, heresies.

Alister McGrath, *The Genesis of Doctrine* (Oxford: Basil
Blackwell, 1990). A heavy but stimulating book based
on his Bampton Lectures; tackles modern liberal thinking head-on; good on the relationship of scripture and
doctrine; dreadfully expensive (get your library to stock
it, and ensure your minister gets a copy).

Bruce Milne, *Know the Truth* (Leicester: Inter-Varsity
Press, 1982). An excellent and readable account of basic
Bible doctrine.

Donald Allister is rector of Cheadle, Cheshire, having
served churches in Hyde, Sevenoaks and Birkenhead since
his ordination in 1976. In the early 1980s he was consultant
editor of the *Church of England Newspaper*, for which he
wrote articles, columns and editorials. He is the author
of *Sickness and Healing in the Church* (Latimer House),
an editor of *Evangel*, and has contributed to several
other books and journals. A vice-chairman of the Church
Society, he is also a member of the Church of England
Evangelical Council and of its theology group.

3

Doctrine and Experience

David Prior

The longest journey in the world is from the head to the heart. This maxim, much beloved of preachers and others, is often quoted to draw a distinction between what we believe in our minds and what we feel in our hearts. Clearly there can be a wide gulf between the two. Our convictions and our knowledge about God may lead us to say one thing; our experience of God may tell us and others something entirely different. For example, many know that God is love, but their experience (or sometimes their lack of experience) appears to contradict what they believe in their minds.

I think of a woman, brought up in a strongly Christian family, who cannot remember a time when she has not wanted to follow Christ and do his will. This desire has, over the years, made her – and her husband – punctilious to the point of punishing herself for not doing as much as she can to please God. She is aware, in her head, of God's accepting love whatever she does or fails to do for him. But she has been operating for years on the 'heart' belief that, because none of us *deserves* God's goodness and blessing, she cannot expect God to bless her with anything she, deep down, longs to experience. Instead of striving to do things for

God, she actually needs to let God do things for her – and in her.

This distinction between head and heart is frequently transposed into a distinction between doctrine and experience. With our heads, so it is said, we grasp what we are taught about God; in our hearts we grasp the reality of God in personal experience. There are also many who affirm that it is to the heart that God reveals himself in a personal way, but that the mind – with all its queries, provisos and rationalisations – often presents a blockage to this revelation.

There are many variations on this theme, but a closer inspection of the scriptures would indicate that all these distinctions – or rather this cluster of distinctions – are barely sustainable in any biblical sense. One of the main reasons for this is that in biblical terminology the 'heart' does not normally exclude the mind, but describes a person in all their capacities and functions. Biblically, therefore, the heart includes the mind and is rarely depicted as distinct from the mind.

When distinctions *are* made, it is in contexts which stress the whole person – for example, when God gives the command to love him with all our heart, soul, mind and strength (Mark 12:30; cf. Deut. 6:5). The distinction, in this case, falls away in the experience of being freed into glad obedience as a person made whole.

When biblical writers are concerned with experience, they describe the whole person experiencing God. The most pervasive and powerful word for this experience of God is to *know* God. The interaction of doctrine and experience is, I believe, best understood by following this particular word and word-group through both the Old Testament and the New Testament. Doctrine and experience are both, after all, pathways to knowledge. Otherwise, we end up forming definitions both of doctrine and of experience based on our own world-view, only to find that these two neat categories are either non-existent in the scriptures, or are incapable of holding the full richness of scriptural truth.

The Garden of Eden

Let us start at the beginning. In the book of Genesis we are introduced to 'the tree of the knowledge of good and evil'. The Lord God instructs Adam, 'you must not eat from' this tree (Gen. 2:17). To do so – as the serpent understood – would produce human beings who would become 'like one of us, knowing good and evil' (Gen. 3:22). A perfect relationship between human beings and their creator did not involve that kind of knowledge. Our fallen condition *does* include such knowledge, but is excluded from that intimate personal relationship which is at the heart of God's purpose in making us in his image. In the language of Genesis 3, fallen human beings now have access to the tree of the knowledge of good and evil, but are excluded from access to the tree of life. We know a lot of things, but we do not know life as God intended: we do not know God.

The next use of the word in the Genesis account is equally significant. In Genesis 4:1 we read that 'Adam lay with [knew] his wife Eve, and she became pregnant and gave birth to Cain.' The word occurs twice more in Genesis 4. This is probably the most significant and seminal use of the word 'know' in the Old Testament. It is both very evocative and very direct, describing the most intimate personal relationship possible between human beings. It is this sense of the word 'know' which captures the heart of the relationship between God and his people. This is stressed most powerfully by prophets such as Jeremiah, Ezekiel and Hosea. All three men liken the relationship between God and his people to the relationship between husband and wife. To know God and to be known by God is like a marriage. The people of Israel constantly corrupted this married relationship by committing adultery with other gods. The results are devastating. In Jeremiah 4:22, the Lord declares, 'My people . . . do not know me.' In Hosea 5:3–4, the Lord says, 'I know all about Ephraim . . . They do not acknowledge the Lord.'

Betrothed to the Lord

The importance of this language becomes clear when God's intention of setting up a new covenant with his people comes into focus. For example, in Hosea 2:19–20 God promises, 'I will betroth you to me for ever; I will betroth you in righteousness and justice, in love and compassion. I will betroth you in faithfulness, and you will acknowledge [know] the Lord.' And in Jeremiah 31:31–4 the prophet proclaims the Lord's intention to make a new covenant with his people:

> 'not . . . like the covenant I made with their forefathers
> . . . because they broke my covenant, though I was a
> husband to them . . . I will put my law in their minds
> and write it on their hearts. I will be their God, and
> they will be my people. No longer will a man teach
> his neighbour, or a man his brother, saying, "Know
> the Lord," because they will all know me, from the
> least of them to the greatest,' declares the Lord. 'For
> I will forgive their wickedness and will remember their
> sins no more.'

It is important to recognise that there were individuals under the old covenant who knew God in this way. It was spasmodic, fleeting and limited. Abraham, God's friend (cf. Isa. 41:8; Jas. 2:23), enjoyed such a personal relationship. David was probably the person who most dramatically scaled the heights and plumbed the depths in thus knowing God. Certainly we have a fuller written record of his experience than of most others, especially in his psalms. The possibility of such knowledge of God was available to all who would set themselves to know him. Those who did so surely found him – and the reality of their experience was expressed in behaviour which demonstrated the character of God. For example, King Josiah 'did what was right and just . . . Is that not what it means to know me?' (Jer. 22:15–16). The best and highest desires of God's people are expressed in the words of Hosea, 'Let us acknowledge [know] the Lord; let us press on to acknowledge [know] him' (Hos. 6:3).

The book of the law

The touchstone for knowing God under the old covenant was the book of the law given through Moses. The whole book of Deuteronomy is presented as what Moses taught Israel (e.g., Deut. 4:1, 5, 14). The scribes, those who studied and taught the book of the law, had a crucial part to play in keeping the requirements of the law before the people. Jehoshaphat, for example, 'sent his officials . . . to teach in the towns of Judah . . . taking with them the Book of the Law of the Lord' (2 Chron. 17:7–9). Ezra is portrayed to us as a teacher of the law (see especially Ezra 7). The single most eloquent testimony to the attractive power of the law remains Psalm 119, an acrostic poem based on the Hebrew alphabet and containing such passionate declarations as 'Oh, how I love your law! I meditate on it all day long' (v. 97) and 'Your word is a lamp to my feet and a light for my path' (v. 105). A similar declaration is made by the author of Psalm 71, who in old age testifies: 'Since my youth, O God, you have taught me' (v. 17).

Nevertheless, however important and esteemed the role of such teachers, and however precious at times the book of the law became to certain people, it is steadily acknowledged in the Old Testament that such 'external' teaching can only last so long and go so far. The problem is classically expressed in Isaiah 29:13 – 'These people come near to me with their mouth and honour me with their lips, but their hearts are far from me. Their worship of me is made up only of rules taught by men.' In the prophecy of Jeremiah the Lord makes the same lament: 'They turned their backs to me and not their faces; though I taught them again and again, they would not listen or respond to discipline' (Jer. 32:33).

It is left to that mighty man of the Old Testament scriptures, the apostle Paul, to summarise both the inadequacy of the old covenant and the real heart of it. In Romans 2:17ff. Paul is speaking to all Jews in their insistence on the permanence of the old covenant. He says:

> . . . if you call yourself a Jew; if you rely on the law and brag about your relationship to God; if you know his will and approve of what is superior because you are instructed by the law; if you are convinced that you are a guide for the blind, a light for those who are in the dark, an instructor of the foolish, a teacher of infants, because you have in the law the embodiment of knowledge and truth – you, then, who teach others, do you not teach yourself? . . .
>
> A man is not a Jew if he is only one outwardly . . . a man is a Jew if he is one inwardly; and circumcision is circumcision of the heart, by the Spirit, not by the written code. (Rom. 2:17–21, 28–9)

Paul then summarises the only true knowledge which the law can bring, in this devastating statement – 'through the law we become conscious of sin' (Rom 3:20). The fact that the law leads to knowledge of sin, not knowledge of God in the true sense, brings Paul to say later of his fellow Jews – 'they are zealous for God, but their zeal is not based on knowledge . . . they did not know the righteousness that comes from God' (Rom. 10:2–3).

Learning to walk

None of these perspectives on the old covenant, the law of the Lord, should allow us to forget that God was continuously teaching his people, in daily experience, what was meant by knowing him and what was involved in knowing him – 'It was I who taught Ephraim to walk' (Hos. 11:3). Moses explained to the people (Deut. 8:3) that God had 'humbled you, causing you to hunger and then feeding you with manna . . . to teach you that man does not live on bread alone but on every word that comes from the mouth of the Lord'. In Isaiah 48:17 we read, 'This is what the Lord says – your Redeemer, the Holy One of Israel: "I am the Lord your God, who teaches you what is best for you, who leads you in the way you should go."'

In the Old Testament we often read of a time that is coming when God's teaching and his people's knowledge will come together in a wholly new way. For example, in Isaiah 30:20 we read,

> Although the Lord gives you the bread of adversity and the water of affliction, your teachers will be hidden no more; with your own eyes you will see them. Whether you turn to the right or to the left, your ears will hear a voice behind you, saying, 'This is the way; walk in it.'

The people of God encouraged one another in Isaiah 2:3, 'Come, let us go up to the mountain of the Lord . . . He will teach us his ways, so that we may walk in his paths.'

The Lord even uses an ass to make this reality come alive to Balaam, who describes himself (Num. 24:16) as 'one who hears the words of God, and has knowledge from the Most High, who sees a vision from the Almighty, who falls prostrate, and whose eyes are opened'. This is the knowledge, this is the teaching, this is the vision of God to which the old covenant could only allude, but which has been made gloriously and universally available in the new covenant.

Forgiveness for deliberate sin

When we come to consider the *new* covenant, it is clear that an entirely new relationship between God and his people is now made possible, a one-to-one relationship. The old covenant did not clearly provide for the forgiveness of sin committed deliberately and with premeditation. When David deliberately committed adultery with Bathsheba and organised the murder of her husband, Uriah, he was eventually brought to a place of repentance and an experience of forgiveness. This gracious act of God was fully in line with his revealed character, but not part of his actual covenant with his people. This is spelled out in Numbers 15:31, for example, where it is made plain that such iniquity is a deliberate rejection of the covenant-love of God: 'his guilt remains on him'. Forgiveness of sin is therefore the bottom line of the new covenant, on the basis of which anyone may know God in personal experience as Father, Teacher and Redeemer.

The basis of this new, personal relationship with God is the atoning death of God's own and only Son, Jesus Christ. The relationship is created and kept alive by the Holy Spirit of God, the Spirit who dwelt in Jesus and who sustained his own relationship with God the Father. Because for us forgiveness of sin is the critical issue of our relationship with God through this new covenant, we must make sure it remains firmly in place in all the ways in which this relationship is worked out – in our own lives and in ministry to others.

How do we do this? At this stage it is necessary to face up honestly to the necessary element of *mystery* in the outworkings of the new covenant. The way that God works within an individual by his Spirit is inevitably and properly unique, hidden, and to that extent mysterious. Because it is all these things, there are endless possibilities for wandering off course into secret and special avenues of purported enlightenment.

It is not surprising, therefore, to find that the earliest and most pervasive heresy in the Christian church arose from claims to such special knowledge of God. These claims could be tested only with great difficulty. Because they revolved around personal, private experiences of knowing God, the umbrella-word for such teachings and tendencies was Gnosticism, which is taken from the Greek word for knowledge, *gnosis*.

Early forms of Gnosticism, which has always had its contemporary examples (not least in ideas current in the mishmash of New Age teachings), would never have had any credibility unless they had been fairly approximate to the truth of the gospel. It is arguable that, except in certain way-out elements, the core of Gnostic teaching was so close to the true gospel that relatively uninstructed believers would have had difficulty drawing any significant distinction between them.

Taught by God

Jesus himself stated unequivocally (John 6:44–5), 'No-one can come to me unless the Father . . . draws him, and I will raise him up on the last day. It is written in the Prophets: "They will all be taught by God." Everyone who listens to the Father and learns from him comes to me.' This personal experience of being drawn by the Father, of hearing and learning from the Father, is clearly seen by Jesus to be normal and necessary in the way individuals come to him as Saviour and Lord. Four crisp statements encapsulate this personal relationship with Jesus as Lord and God: 'you will know the truth, and the truth will set you free' (John 8:32); 'I am the way and the truth and the life. No-one comes to the Father except through me' (John 14:6); 'if the Son sets you free, you will be free indeed' (John 8:36); 'the truth . . . is in Jesus' (Eph. 4:21).

All the Johannine writings (i.e., Gospel, Epistles and Apocalypse) make full use of the cluster of Greek words for *know* and *knowledge*. In an important passage where he is appealing to his readers not to be drawn aside into false doctrine, John stresses with some passion that they have already been enlightened to the point where further teaching appears less than imperative. John is obviously not downgrading a ministry which he himself is, at that very time, strongly and clearly pursuing with them; but he does say, 'I am writing these things to you about those who are trying to lead you astray. As for you, the anointing you received from him remains in you, and you do not need anyone to teach you. But as his anointing teaches you about all things and as that anointing is true, not counterfeit – just as it has taught you, remain in him' (1 John 2:26–7). In a previous verse in the same chapter (v. 20) John appears – on one reading of the text – to say that, as a result of having been thus anointed by the Holy One, 'you know everything'. A more likely rendering is 'all of you know', as foretold in Jeremiah (31:34) when explaining the new covenant, 'No longer will a man teach his neighbour . . . saying, "Know the Lord," because they will all know me.'

This remarkable assertion by John is presumably based on the promises made by Jesus to his disciples just before his death, that 'the Holy Spirit . . . will teach you all things . . . When the Spirit of truth comes, he will guide you into all truth' (John 14:26; 16:13). This essential and distinctive activity of God under the new covenant is noted, almost in passing, by Paul in 1 Thessalonians 4:9, when he says: 'Now about brotherly love we do not need to write to you, for you yourselves have been taught by God to love each other.' This love for one another in the body of Christ is at the heart of the new covenant; it is, in fact, the 'new commandment' given by Jesus to his disciples (John 13:34–5) – a new and challenging application, modelled by Jesus himself, of the old commandment to love God and our neighbour (cf. 1 John 2:7–8). Christians in Thessalonica had been taught by God to walk in such mutual love – clear evidence that they knew God.

It must be significant that Paul, having acknowledged that God himself had taught the Christians in Thessalonica to love one another, still urges them to do so 'more and more'. Exhortation has its rightful place; but no human being can engender such mutual love in a church by teaching people about love, let alone by beating them over the heads with the new commandment. It is easy for an over-conscientious pastor to lay a guilt-trip on people, with a plethora of 'oughts' and 'ought nots'. When *God* teaches a church to love one another, it is manifest, beautiful and supernatural. It does not need much urging to do so more and more: instead of being a burden and a problem, the new commandment has become a delight – we cannot have too much of it. It is not surprising, therefore, that Paul explains that insisting on the letter of the law is to deal in death and to revert to the old covenant: we are called to be competent ministers of the new covenant of life in the Spirit (2 Cor. 3:6).

At this stage we need to remind ourselves that John insists that all claims to know God in personal experience must be properly tested. This is particularly important in a climate like the one prevalent today in the West. Thirty years ago, Francis Schaeffer warned that 'The end of the twentieth century will be a time of contentless mysticism.' All spiritual experiences need to be evaluated. John's touchstone was clear:

> Dear Friends, do not believe every spirit, but test the spirits to see whether they are from God, because many false prophets have gone out into the world. This is how you can recognise the Spirit of God: Every spirit that acknowledges that Jesus Christ has come in the flesh is from God, but every spirit that does not acknowledge Jesus is not from God. (1 John 4:1–3)

In the language of Paul, the test of anyone's spiritual experience is whether a person is willing and able to say 'Jesus is Lord' (1 Cor. 12:3) – and give evidence for it, not least in the face of persecution.

Among the questions set in the logic paper in my final examinations at university, I found the following gem: 'Is it possible for me to have your chicken-pox?' Forty-five minutes were allowed to write an answer. A correct answer would have been something like this, suitably padded out: your chicken-pox is yours and my chicken-pox is mine; I do not have yours and you do not have mine; but what we have in common is chicken-pox. Without reducing experience of God to logical absurdity, I cannot have your experience of God and you cannot have mine; but what you and I have in common is Jesus Christ as Lord – we are one in him. If either you or I actually do not have Jesus Christ as Lord, whatever either of us may claim, we cannot know that oneness.

All in all, both John and Paul place immense confidence in the radical and fundamental transformation brought about in a person who is born again by God's Spirit, becomes a child of God and a new creation in Christ, is forgiven all their sin, and experiences the indwelling work of God's Spirit.

Teaching and learning

It can be seen that Christian teaching/doctrine is clearly for disciples of Jesus Christ, those 'taught by God'. The words *doctrine* and *disciple* both come from Latin roots, the first meaning *teaching* and the second meaning *learner*. The aim of teaching or doctrine, therefore, must be to increase the learning of the disciple – not learning in a cerebral vacuum, but learning which deepens discipleship.

Recently, a person experienced in Christian education discussed with our staff-team priorities for equipping potential leadership teams for more substantial ministry. One particular observation struck home: 'You are clearly a teaching church, but are you a learning church?' It was a searching question. It probably exposes the wide gap between what is taught and what is learned, between doctrine and discipleship.

This principle Jesus himself enunciated when he noted that 'A student is not above his teacher, nor a servant above his master: it is enough for the student to be like his teacher, and the servant like his master' (Matt. 10:24–5). In Luke 6:40 Jesus says in similar vein – 'everyone who is fully trained will be like his teacher.' Thus, the purpose of such teaching is to make disciples like Jesus.

The net implications of these perspectives are reasonably clear: Christian doctrine is for Christian disciples. Christian disciples are those who know what it is to be forgiven, what it is to have received the anointing of the Holy Spirit, and what it is to be daily led by the Spirit. Christian teaching must always give high profile to – and never silently assume – this firm foundation of assured forgiveness and the internal operation of the Spirit. As Christian disciples daily seek to follow Jesus Christ as Lord, it is essential to do so with the goal and intention of being made like him. As Christian disciples thus become like Jesus Christ, being changed into his likeness through the work of the Spirit from one degree of glory to another (2 Cor. 3:18), so we come to know God more and more. We come to know that love which surpasses knowledge (Eph. 3:19); we come to know Christ himself in the power of his resurrection and in the fellowship of his sufferings (Phil. 3:10).

Paul looks forward to the time when 'I shall know fully, even as I am fully known' (1 Cor. 13:12). What it means to be 'fully known' by God is beautifully expressed by David in Psalm 139:1–6:

> O Lord, you have searched me
> and you know me.
> You know when I sit and when I rise;
> you perceive my thoughts from afar.
> You discern my going out and my lying down;
> you are familiar with all my ways.
>
> Before a word is on my tongue
> you know it completely, O Lord.
>
> You hem me in – behind and before;
> you have laid your hand upon me.
> Such knowledge is too wonderful for me,
> too lofty for me to attain.

Paul expects one day to attain such knowledge – the process has already begun: 'God . . . made his light shine in our hearts to give the light of the knowledge of the glory of God in the face of Christ' (2 Cor. 4:6). Indeed, all the great prayers of Paul for his readers emphasise his concern that they should come to and increase in the knowledge of God and of his Son Jesus Christ (Eph. 1:15–21; 3:14–19; Phil. 1:9–11; Col. 1:9–14; cf. Eph. 4:13; Col. 3:10). All this is precisely what Zechariah prophesied over his son John (the Baptist), saying 'and you, my child, will be called the prophet of the Most High; for you will go on before the Lord to prepare the way for him, to give his people the knowledge of salvation through the forgiveness

of their sins, because of the tender mercy of our God'
(Luke 1:76–8).

A deposit of truth

It becomes very clear, in the light of the above, why the
first Christian disciples found it impossible to grow up as
disciples of Christ and to become like Christ without being
grounded in certain fundamentals. Luke describes these
fundamentals in Acts 2:42 – 'They devoted themselves
to the apostles' teaching and to the fellowship, to the
breaking of bread and to prayer.' Having received the
forgiveness of sins, having been filled with the Holy Spirit,
having been baptised in the name of Jesus Christ, these
first Christian disciples were completely committed to this
interwoven pattern of discipleship. The teaching needed
the fellowship, and the fellowship needed the teaching.
The teaching and the fellowship needed the worship, the
worship needed the teaching and the fellowship. The
teaching, the fellowship and the worship needed a rhythm
and discipline of prayer together: prayer together needed
the context of teaching, fellowship, and worship. This balanced and rounded experience of Christian community-life
led to growing maturity in Christian disciples, a growth
which included sharing Christ with outsiders.

The teaching of the apostles inevitably became a coherent deposit of truth, which was consistently applied into
the life of the emerging Christian churches throughout the
Mediterranean. To this the Pastoral Epistles give eloquent
testimony, not least in their strong distinction between
sound doctrine and false doctrine.

Writing to a relatively young leader, Timothy, Paul
stresses the fundamental importance of this teaching:
'What you heard from me, keep as the pattern of sound
teaching, with faith and love in Christ Jesus. Guard the
good deposit that was entrusted to you – guard it with
the help of the Holy Spirit who lives in us' (2 Tim. 1:13).
Paul's emphasis on faith, love and the help of the Holy
Spirit roots this guardianship of doctrine deeply in the

new covenant. We may compare Paul's gratitude, as he reflects on the experience of Christians in Rome, when he says: 'Thanks be to God that . . . you wholeheartedly obeyed the form of teaching to which you were entrusted' (Rom. 6:17).

Holy and healthy lives

Paul's insistence on such wholehearted obedience is another feature of the Pastoral Epistles, with their emphasis on sheer quality of behaviour. There is, in these epistles, no such thing as sound teaching without healthy living. If teaching does not lead to healthy living, then the teaching is not truly sound, nor is it distinctively Christian. God the Holy Spirit is the only truly Christian teacher (i.e., teacher of Christ). If we relegate the Holy Spirit to the sidelines, either by neglect or by taking him for granted instead of directly and continuously inviting him to be the teacher, we have slipped back under the old covenant.

Perhaps this is why Jesus warned his own disciples against trends prevalent among the Pharisees, those fierce guardians of the old covenant. He said: 'You are not to be called "Rabbi", for you have only one Master and you are all brothers' (Matt. 23:8). It is all too easy to replace a rabbi with a Christian guru.

This is not merely a matter of the methods we use, or even of ensuring that what and when we teach is rooted in daily life and in a worshipping community. We have not been involved in *Christian* teaching if we have merely passed on information. Information was an essential part – and a fatal limitation – of the *old* covenant. The *new* covenant is concerned with and actively contributes to the *formation* of disciples.

We need to add that it is only as Christians live lives which are consistent with their faith in Christ, being formed as disciples of Christ, that they are competent to teach others. Paul makes that plain in writing to the Romans (15:14) – 'you . . . are full of goodness, complete in knowledge and competent to instruct one another'.

Such consistency in daily behaviour, as the fruit of true knowledge of God, includes the readiness to be taught, even or especially if we are called to teach. There are many who are, frankly, unteachable – not because of incompetence on the part of those teaching, but because the person refuses to learn or even to listen.

I recently heard about the impact of one such man on a whole church where he was a member of staff. Time after time he treated others with insensitivity and arrogance. Though presented, gently but firmly, over a long period of time with the impact of his behaviour, he refused to acknowledge that any fault lay with him, or that he needed to change and be changed. Neither confrontation nor exhortation cut any ice. He left that church with a trail of heartbreak, if not havoc, behind him.

Moving from unbelief

What about Christian doctrine and teaching for those who are outside the church and the faith? Is it impossible for an unbeliever truly to understand Christian teaching, if there needs to be experience of new birth and new life in Christ before Christian teaching can be taken on board? Jesus gives us an important perspective on this problem when he says, in debate with questioning Jews, 'If anyone chooses to do God's will, he will find out whether my teaching comes from God or whether I speak on my own' (John 7:17). Mere curiosity or passing whim will not bring a person to know God. Unbelievers need a full-blooded, challenging and compassionate apologetic for the Christian faith, but there also needs to be a deliberate choice by an unbeliever to seek out the will of God in order to do it. This is the principle, valid for actual as well as for possible disciples of Christ, spelled out by James: 'humbly accept the word planted in you, which can save you' (Jas. 1:21).

This is also the challenge of *parables* in the public teaching of Jesus. Only if individuals or groups (as exemplified by 'the disciples') pursued him privately, did Jesus lead them into personal encounter with and experience of God. When the disciples asked, 'Why do you speak to the people in parables?', he replied, 'The knowledge of the secrets of the kingdom of heaven has been given to you, but not to them' (Matt. 13:10–11).

Paul writes on one occasion (2 Cor. 10:4–5): 'The weapons we fight with . . . have divine power to demolish strongholds. We demolish arguments and every pretension that sets itself up against the knowledge of God.' We must, then, mobilise these resources – what Paul calls elsewhere 'the full armour of God' (Eph. 6:13–17) – in discussing Jesus Christ with unbelievers. Unless we do use these special resources, or 'weapons', people remain safe – but lost – within the sturdy walls of their own theories and convictions, by which they buttress their chosen lifestyle.

We are also called to demonstrate the distinctive attractiveness of an alternative daily lifestyle – one which gives the answer to corruption, cynicism and self-centredness. The beauty of such holiness is a part (an essential part) of Christian apologetics. As Paul again puts it – 'God . . . always leads us in triumphal procession in Christ and through us spreads everywhere the fragrance of the knowledge of him' (2 Cor. 2:14). In fact, Paul maintains that this is the authentic ministry of those who know God personally through Christ under the terms of the new covenant (cf. 2 Cor. 3:1ff.). That is why such fragrance is, at one and the same time, both irresistible and repugnant: it attracts the serious seeker and repels the superficial sceptic.

It is important that we are under no illusions concerning the blindness, both in scale and in intensity, experienced by unbelievers. Paul puts it this way: 'although they knew God, they neither glorified him as God nor gave thanks to him, but their thinking became futile and their foolish hearts were darkened' (Rom. 1:21). It needs a miracle, therefore, if light is to shine into such darkness, so that individuals experience a second birth.

It is self-evident that nobody comes to know God through their own wisdom or knowledge (cf. 1 Cor. 1:21). Nevertheless, we as believers are commissioned with the task and the privilege of being the Lord's servants to unbelievers. But, as Paul reminded Timothy, 'the Lord's servant must not quarrel; instead he must be kind to everyone, able to teach, not resentful. Those who oppose him he must gently instruct, in the hope that God will grant them repentance leading them to a knowledge of the truth, and that they will come to their senses and escape from the trap of the devil, who has taken them captive to do his will' (2 Tim. 2:24–6). The grip of Satan on the minds and lives of unbelievers underlines the importance of their experiencing the reality of God in Christ in a way which affects them as persons – in their thinking, feeling and doing – not only challenging the way they think or simply touching their emotions.

Thinking and feeling

It can now be seen that doctrine and experience are not two parts or halves of what it is to be Christian. Experience cannot be limited to what our emotions or our feelings tell us. Experience includes *both* the thinking contents of our minds *and* the feeling contents of our emotions. It also includes what is subconscious, intuitive, repressed, forgotten, unacknowledged or unexplained. We should never, therefore, allow any dichotomy between what we are taught/learn through our minds and what our feelings/instincts teach us. They should, rather, be allowed to interact with each other under the scrutiny of the scriptures, so that we gradually think as God thinks and feel as God feels.

In ministry to others we must not attempt to play God. It is *his* work to bring people to assurance of forgiveness. We must not railroad the creative work of his indwelling Holy Spirit in individuals. A person can, under the influence of strong personalities or the pressure of circumstances, be presented with a package of right beliefs, to which they then subscribe verbally in a series of correct statements. It is crucial not to assume that such mental assent necessarily indicates the work of the Spirit in a person. Rather, we must pray for discernment to recognise God at work; we must pray for sensitivity in bringing relevant teaching to bear on the daily experience of Christian disciples; we must pray for appropriate wisdom concerning unbelievers in their actual situation and their deep-down attitudes towards God. Yes, we must *pray*. When not sure what or how to teach, we must pray. When we *are* sure, we must pray. The very act of prayer is a statement that we depend on God's Holy Spirit.

If this is a correct understanding of the interaction between doctrine and experience, we all need to master the scriptures and to be mastered by the Holy Spirit – not to presume the first, or to assume the second: but to apply ourselves to both. This is the way to know God – or, in the self-adjustment made by Paul, to be known by God (Gal. 4:9). This is the way to help others to know God and be known by God. This is the way for us all to grow in knowing God and in being known by God.

Questions for Discussion

1. How can my church more effectively integrate the four key ingredients mentioned in Acts 2:42 (i.e., teaching, fellowship, worship and prayer)?

2. A member of my church announces a personal decision with the remark, 'The Lord has told me that . . . ' How do I react to this? Is it right to question the decision? What biblical insights and perspectives might be relevant?

3. What signs indicate that a person is being drawn by the Father? How can scriptural teaching be best

brought and applied to a person's life when God is thus at work?

4. Is there a place for teaching doctrine simply as information? Is it valuable to store up a body of knowledge about God? What are the dangers in so doing? Is it right to take such risks? Is it worth it?

5. Why is it important to establish in each situation that a person is firmly assured of forgiveness from God? What happens when someone, even a clear believer, is not sure of God's forgiveness?

6. What practical steps can I take (a) to respect the supreme work of the Holy Spirit as Teacher, (b) to help others recognise and respond to the Holy Spirit?

For further reading

Gerard Hughes, *God of Surprises* (London: Darton, Longman & Todd, 1985)

J. I. Packer, *Knowing God* (London: Hodder & Stoughton, 1973)

Brother Ramon, *Deeper into God* (London: Marshall Pickering, 1991)

Brother Ramon, *Heaven on Earth* (London: Marshall Pickering, 1991)

T. A. Smail, *Reflected Glory* (London: Hodder & Stoughton, 1975)

David Prior. After a curacy in the diocese of Southwark, he spent seven years in a multiracial parish in Cape Town. Five years as Vicar of St Aldate's, Oxford, were followed by a year's sabbatical in the USA. In 1985 he moved to his present work in London as Vicar of St Michael's Chester Square and priest-in-charge of Christ Church Mayfair. He retains close links with Africa and Latin America. He has written several books, including *The Message of 1 Corinthians*, The Bible Speaks Today Series (Leicester: IVP, 1985) and *Jesus and Power*, The Jesus Library (London: Hodder & Stoughton, 1986).

4

Doctrine and Evangelism

Gavin Reid

Two recently published, and very significant, books about evangelism bemoan the lack of contact between those who enthuse about evangelism and those who take theology seriously. William Abraham opens his crucial study *The Logic of Evangelism* with the words: 'One of the undeniable features of modern theology is the scant attention it has given to the topic of evangelism. It is virtually impossible to find a critical, in-depth study of the subject by a major theologian.'[1] And Bishop Michael Marshall, in *The Gospel Connection*, takes up Abraham's lament at the start of his second chapter. 'Surely', he writes, 'the theologians need the evangelists and the evangelists need the theologians.' However, Marshall moves on to a critical reflection on trends in Western theology:

> The theologians most certainly need the evangelists. For too long we have assumed that theology is a specialist branch of philosophy concerned with ideas about God. Hence the reduction of Christianity into yet another ideology . . . theology has become primarily an activity of the mind tested in the laboratory of the debating chamber, the lecture room, or those interminable discussion groups![2]

While I consider Marshall's criticisms a shade unkind and over-generalised, it is certainly an impression that can easily be gained, and thus it is small wonder that those who have great enthusiasms about their own discovery of the gospel are hardly likely to look to theologians for help, either with their own understandings or in the task of sharing their discovery with others.

Evangelism, therefore, is often regarded as the preserve of enthusiasts, and enthusiasm is not usually seen as linked to reflection and thought. While there is some truth in that caricature, it is ultimately unfair. But caricaturing affects the other side of the story also. Granted that theology and 'doctrine' are not exactly the same thing, the way we do theology in the West has affected the way we often write off 'doctrine' as somewhat removed from the realities of life and faith. We too easily regard a concern for doctrine to be the preserve of religious equivalents of 'barrack-room lawyers'. Doctrine, on this view, is dull stuff about print and propositions. It is the language – so some would say – of those who want to criticise and split hairs. Nobody was ever converted by reciting creeds at them or quoting chunks out of the Thirty-nine Articles.

This caricaturing on both sides is aided and abetted by a trend which has been more obvious in recent years – the emphasis upon experience. The charismatic movement has been a much-needed liberation from dry, cerebral Christianity which was strong on doctrinal or liturgical correctness while weak, and even repressive, on emotion and the experiential. If Christians are people who have been set free from a crippling bondage and have been forgiven and assured of the neverending love of God, how can they talk or sing about such realities as if they were chanting details from a telephone directory?

There is now much more of a place for the experiential in contemporary spirituality – whether it be in expressions of joy or whether it be in recognitions of vulnerability. However, as usually happens, every basically healthy development carries a danger. The danger with the emphasis upon feelings is that we disregard the rational. Doctrine is to do with the rational – but unless there are good reasons for our feelings, we are living unreal lives. Ultimately doctrine matters. It is not enough to say, 'Smile, God loves you.' At some point we have to say why we have grounds for believing and sharing such a sentiment.

In reality doctrine and experience are close relations. Doctrine emerges as people make sense of what they have discovered. The Bible is a book full of discoveries and experiences. It is about what people have learned about God as a result of experiencing him at work. Above all, it is about understanding the implications of the birth, life, death and resurrection of Jesus. And in saying this, we are right at the heart of the business of evangelism, for, as the Church of England report *The Measure of Mission* affirms: 'We are charged to communicate that the life, death and resurrection of Jesus Christ is good news from God.'[3]

Doctrine and conversion

Is evangelism therefore to be considered as the communication of right doctrine? If we get it right, is that the secret of 'bringing people to faith'? The answer to this question is surprisingly complex, for two reasons.

The first reason is that of the Holy Spirit. 'The wind', said Jesus in his famous conversation with Nicodemus, 'blows wherever it pleases . . . So it is with everyone born of the Spirit' (John 3:8). There can be little doubt that people come to faith in Christ in some pretty odd ways! Very often there appears to be no doctrine whatsoever involved. One person I have met came to Christ in a foxhole in the Second World War. As bullets flew overhead, he knew he needed a saviour in every sense – especially the physical! Others find it difficult to specify any particular moment as the moment of their conversion. For them, discovering Christ was a gentle process over many years. All one can conclude is that in one way or another the Holy Spirit acted to draw them to Christ.

Here we find ourselves touching upon the second complication. The vast majority of conversions are gentle, and the result of *processes* of discovery rather than any particular *crisis*. They cannot be put down to a formal presentation of the gospel. Although evangelists should indeed take doctrine seriously, many of those who respond, and are therefore counted as converts because of evangelists, did not respond because of the particular message preached. Every evangelist can tell of those who come forward at the end of a sermon and preface their comments by, 'It wasn't anything you said, but . . . ' What has happened is that the Spirit has used the occasion to build on what had probably already been started in the hearts and minds of those who responded. Conversions are rarely simple stories!

This would appear to play down the significance of doctrine, but there is more that should be said. It is true that a majority of converts will claim they were drawn to Christ because of what they saw in other people who believed, but evangelism does not end with attracting people to want to say 'yes'. It ends (if indeed it ever ends, because we spend our whole lives being changed by the gospel) with *nurture*; and nurture is about helping people to realise who it is that they have turned to, what it is they have joined and how it is that they should live. *All this has to do with doctrine*. Much of the great doctrinal material in the New Testament is to be found in the epistles, but they are simply letters to newborn Christians, helping them to grow up in an alien world. In today's church jargon, the epistles are nurture-group material.

The story of Cornelius (Acts 10) is relevant here. It is clear, early in the narrative, that the human side of conversion is in place. Cornelius has obviously turned to God, in spite of all the religious notions of his own culture and upbringing. When Peter eventually meets him he soon recognises that the centurion is accepted by God (v. 35). What the story makes clear, however, is that it was God's will that this person who showed repentance and faith should *understand* who it was that he believed in and what this meant. In other words, he needed nurturing in doctrine. He needed to know all that Peter – a prime witness to the life, death and resurrection of Jesus – had to say.

A right understanding of the church

One of the fundamental problems we face with the encouragement of evangelism is that many in our churches are afraid of the prospect. Evangelism doesn't seem natural to the sort of church they feel they belong to – or want to belong to. Indeed, the idea of 'belonging' to a church is probably alien to many who attend.

A great deal of this can be traced to the Western idea (a particularly English one) that religion is a private matter and that therefore the institutional church exists for the benefit of its consumers. To people with such understandings the challenge of evangelism is not only a threat – it is to confuse things. The 'institution' and its agents may want to propagate their views in society, but it is hardly the task of the consumer-attender. There is a further consequence of this private-view approach to religion. 'Private' is seen to be part of a complex of ideas including reverence and the sacred. In our British culture, what is sacred needs to be spoken about with reticence and reserve. Evangelism – which is often caricatured as a brash and insensitive activity – hardly goes hand-in-hand with what is considered to be an appropriate reticence. God is too sublime to be 'sold', hawked around or commended to others.

St Peter, however, thought otherwise. In the first epistle attributed to him, we read: 'In your hearts set apart [Gk. = sanctify] Christ as Lord. Always be prepared to give an answer to everyone who asks you to give the reason for the hope that you have' (1 Pet. 3:15). This alliance between reverence and witness is a theme of the epistle. Peter – in words echoing phrases from the book of Deuteronomy – reminded his readers that: 'You are a chosen people, a royal priesthood, a holy nation, a people belonging to God, *that you may declare the praises of him*

who called you out of darkness into his wonderful light'
(1 Pet. 2:9, my italics). It is not clear who is meant to be
the listener to these declarations of praise. Is it God, and
are we therefore talking about worship? Or is it men and
women, and are we talking about evangelism?

The truth, almost certainly, is that it is *both*. Witness is
the other side of the coin of worship. It is saying to one's
fellows what one says to God. It is a mark of integrity. How
can one say 'How great thou art' in worship on Sunday and
deny it through silence or even contradiction on Monday
before others?

The link in Peter's mind between the church and the
old covenant people of God was more than a useful
illustration. It was of the *essence*. The old covenant
people of God were *people within a story*. They were
the people who had once been a collection of ill-used
slaves in Egypt, only to be rescued by the intervention of
God. The exodus was more than an episode in the past. It
was a continuing story, ever present in the consciousness
of the people. Whenever the harvest was gathered in, an
offering would be made of the firstfruits, accompanied by
these words:

> My father was a wandering Aramean, and he went
> down into Egypt with a few people and lived there
> and became a great nation, powerful and numerous.
> But the Egyptians ill-treated us and made us suffer,
> putting us to hard labour. Then we cried out to the
> Lord, the God of our fathers, and the Lord heard our
> voice and saw our misery, toil and oppression. So the
> Lord brought us out of Egypt with a mighty hand and an
> outstretched arm, with great terror and with miraculous
> signs and wonders. He brought us to this place and gave
> us this land, a land flowing with milk and honey; and
> now I bring the firstfruits of the soil that you, O Lord,
> have given me. (Deut. 26:5–10)

Should a non-Jew wish to practise the Jewish religion, he
would be circumcised and (certainly by Graeco-Roman

times) *baptised*. The symbolism of being under water and rising alive from it identified the proselyte with the Red Sea *story* of the God who had rescued his people from slavery.

The apostles saw the church in the same light – people of the story. At the last supper, however, Jesus had rewritten the story. Once again a nation had been created by an act of God. The slavery and bondage on this occasion had been to sin and the power of Satan. The act of deliverance was the body given for us and the blood shed for us for the forgiveness of our sins. The Passover and Red Sea crossing elements in the story of the people of the old covenant are merged and replaced by the cross of Calvary and the empty tomb. There is a new story and a new people. The major difference is that whereas there were only hints in the Old Testament that membership of the people of the story might be open to the non-Jew, it was now clear that the membership of the new people of the story was intended to be open to all.

For the Christian community, therefore, the story is more than a constant reminder of the identity of the people of God. The story is the good news that has to be shared, first in Jerusalem, then Samaria and to the ends of the earth (Acts 1:8). The rite of initiation into the people of God is no longer circumcision but *baptism*, a change which reveals that, among other things, there is now no distinction between male and female: ' . . . all of you who were baptised into Christ have clothed yourselves with Christ. There is neither Jew nor Greek, slave nor free, male nor female, for you are all one in Christ Jesus' (Gal. 3:27–8).

Christians, therefore, are the new covenant people of the story. Witness and worship are two sides of the same coin. For the church to be true to itself, it must continue to remind itself of the story of its deliverance. The Holy Communion service is the setting *par excellence* of that continuous retelling.

Writing on Zwingli's theology of the eucharist, Alister McGrath picks up this theme which the Swiss theologian saw and which (even if there is more to the eucharist) surely must hold true: 'Zwingli affirms that the Eucharist narrates the foundational event of the Christian community, and that by doing so, it gives substance to the values and aspirations of that community, and enhances its sense of unity and purpose.'[4] In the same article McGrath quotes some telling words from Alasdair MacIntyre's work *After Virtue*: ' . . . we all live out narratives in our lives and . . . we understand our own lives in terms of narratives that we live out . . . '[5] As people of the story – receiving it from others and seeing ourselves caught up in it – Christians find themselves to be new people with a new identity and purpose in life.

For the church to be true to itself, however, it must also be retelling its story to those outside its membership. It was founded on the work of *apostles* and is itself *apostolic*. It exists not to stand still, but to *go* – not only to listen, but also to tell. Evangelism is therefore an essential element of what the church is and what it is meant to do. Any doctrine of the church that does not see evangelism at the heart of its being is a false doctrine.

Evangelism

Before we can talk meaningfully about the 'place' of doctrine within evangelism, we need to be clear as to the nature of evangelism itself. The suffix 'ism' tends to distort things – it makes evangelism a subject in itself rather than an activity. We tend to use the word in a static rather than a dynamic way. We talk of 'doing' evangelism, when the New Testament simply talks in terms of 'evangelising'. The noun 'evangelism' is relatively new. Its first recorded use, in English, dates to the middle of the seventeenth century.

The New Testament talks about the 'evangel', meaning the content of the story. It talks about 'evangelists', referring to people with a particular gift and calling of story-telling, and it speaks of 'evangelising' as the natural activity of sharing good news – any good news, and the particular good news of Jesus.

It is hard to discern any sense in which the New Testament Christian community felt it was engaging in a special activity by evangelising. What we see is a community of people discovering that they were caught up in the implications of the story of Jesus and recognising that they were called to carry on living out and sharing the story. Peter and John, when urged by the authorities to keep silent, replied: 'Judge for yourselves whether it is right in God's sight to obey you rather than God. For we cannot help speaking about what we have seen and heard' (Acts 4:19–20). Speaking about the story that was taking place around them was part of the *obedience* and integrity of the first Christians.

True evangelism is therefore the healthy and necessary overspill of the story that holds the church together and which gives it a sense of purpose. This means that the story also becomes testimony – *my story*. The distinction that some make between 'doctrine and evangelism', with which I started this essay is, in fact, a false one. My testimony cannot be unrelated to doctrine because it cannot be unrelated to the story of Christ.

It is only when we have established evangelising as the essence of the general life of the church that we can understand evangelism or evangelists. An evangelist is someone with a particular gift for commending the story to others and calling for response. That gift is often tightly bound up with the personal testimony of the evangelist. He or she may well have had a particularly dramatic and sudden conversion – as was the case with St Paul. Because of this the evangelist can see the darkness of life without Christ in greater contrast to the light of life with him. It is perhaps significant that St Paul had a clear sense of his calling at the time of his conversion experience. When he later related his call it was expressed in stark terms: 'I am sending you . . . to open their eyes and turn them from darkness to light, and from the power of Satan to God, so that they may receive forgiveness of sins and a place among those who are sanctified by faith in me' (Acts 26:17–18). The particular evangelism of the evangelist relies on the general ongoing evangelism of the church. In its turn, the particular gift of the evangelist encourages the general evangelism of the church. All gift-ministries have the same effect. The gifts are given not to endue status on the recipient, but grace upon the community. They are given as visual aids and reminders of parts of the continuing agenda.

Evangelists therefore have an important role, but to define evangelism in the light of their particular gift is to distort matters. Evangelism is *not* solely '*preaching* the gospel' – that is the ministry of the evangelist. Evangelism is much more the natural sharing of the story in daily life against the continual hope that increasing numbers of people may discover that the promises and possibilities it contains are for them and their children.

Contemporary, developed urban society, however, does not easily allow relationships to flourish – unlike the case in New Testament times. Life is more structured, and therefore evangelism has no choice but to have to be more structured and even contrived. A group has to be 'set up'. Once upon a time it would just happen. John Wesley could stand in a market-place and shout about Christ and he would draw attention. A meeting would be generated. It was something others would do for other purposes. Today, if someone tried the same tactic they would be drowned by traffic noise, thought to be odd, and probably asked to move on for causing an obstruction. Meetings, today, have to be specially planned.

Because of the necessary contrivedness of so much evangelism – especially the evangelism of evangelists – we can easily lose sight of the essential naturalness of the general evangelism of the people of God. The truth, however, is that the majority of conversions still come as a result of the general witness of the people of God in everyday relationships, rather than the particular ministry of evangelists. *Their story* rubs off on others. It is caught and sensed as much as it is taught and learned.

This being the case – where does 'doctrine' come in within evangelism? If Christianity is caught rather than taught, is there therefore no place for teaching and content? The answer is 'yes', but the question reveals another common misunderstanding. *People rarely convert to Christ through taking in and grasping doctrine*. They turn to the Lord through an attraction to the people of the story. They also turn to Christ because of the inner witness of the Holy Spirit. That turning is real. There is usually a recognition that something *better* has been found than had been found before. Turning may sometimes be the turning of guilt about past and present situations, but it can often be the turning of attraction to the new possibilities. This is why an evangelism which concentrates on trying to create a sense of guilt can be false. Many new Christians only feel guilt later on, when they fully realise the implications of their past way of life in the light of a growing understanding of the holiness of God.

Doctrine in evangelism is not so much what converts as what establishes the new believer. We can see in the case of the woman at the well (John 4) and Cornelius (Acts 10) that the New Testament contains cases of people who became believers before they fully knew *what* to believe. The main lesson to learn from the Cornelius episode is that God does not consider the attitude of readiness to believe to be enough. As we have seen, Peter needed to come to Cornelius to provide the doctrine – to fill out the details of what the centurion was groping towards. Doctrine matters.

Doctrine, evangelism and nurture

Thus far I have tried to look at the doctrines that lie behind the practice of evangelism. I have, in particular, argued that everything hinges on a correct doctrine of the church – one which sees itself as the people of God particularly chosen and called to declare his praises. It is because this biblical understanding is so little recognised that evangelism often becomes an awkward element to put in place.

I have also argued that when we analyse how the

majority of people grasp (and are grasped by) the gospel, we discover that, in practice, evangelism is more complex than the communication of certain doctrines. Nevertheless, because nurture is central to the completion of the evangelising process, doctrine is ultimately vital.

Are there, then, a set of doctrines which – whether at the nurture stage or earlier – must be expounded and understood? The answer has to be in the affirmative. If the church is to be obedient to God, it must witness to the truth about God. We should not set out to evangelise on the basis of 'never mind the quality, feel the width'. Having said this, it does not follow that a person's saved status in the sight of God depends on his or her accurate grasp of a set of necessary doctrines. Probably the vast majority of Christians are, and always have been, imperfect in their understandings.

There is a second reason why we need to think in a thorough way about doctrine within evangelism. Not only is it part of our obedience to God to attempt to speak the truth about him, it is – said Christ – the truth that sets us free (John 8:32). Doctrine affects our spiritual health.

What, then, are the doctrines at the heart of the witness and nurture within the evangelism process? In the 1968 report of the Evangelical Alliance Commission on Evangelism there was an attempt to trim things down to an 'irreducible minimum':

The ingredients of the Gospel as given, though they fall far short of even a full outline, are nonetheless more than is required for saving faith. Yet the attempt to define the irreducible minimum which is essential for saving faith is fraught with danger, for brevity too easily leads to obscurity. It is necessary, however, to summarise that minimum for the sake of later sections of the Report, and at the same time to emphasise that the summary must be understood in the light of the fuller statements already made.

The first essential is belief in Jesus Christ as both fully man and fully God. The second is a realistic understanding of the plight of man as a helpless sinner before a Holy God. The third essential is belief in the atoning death and triumphant resurrection of Christ as the sole means of a man's redemption from sin and reconciliation to God. The fourth essential is the response to the work of the Holy Spirit, the response of repentance and faith as a genuine turning from sin and an act of trust in God.[6]

These words set out a crisp and helpful summary of the gospel as it has been preached by evangelicals for many years. However, it suffers from the besetting failure of much evangelical evangelising. The message – although it starts with Christ – is essentially man-centred. It pictures God as completely focused on redeeming individual people. It fails to do justice to the great theme at the heart of Christ's teaching – the kingdom of God. William Abraham in *The Logic of Evangelism* opens his chapter on 'The Gospel' with an insistence that our message has to centre not on humanity's need, but on God's reigning activity:

Any vision of evangelism that ignores the Kingdom of God, or relegates it to a position of secondary importance or fails to wrestle thoroughly with its content, is destined at the outset to fail . . .
What is at stake is the fundamental theological horizon within which both Jesus and his followers conceive and carry out the first, and paradigmatic, evangelistic action of the church.[7]

I have personally found it helpful to base a nurture course for new Christians and serious seekers on the Lord's Prayer. It means that we have to start positioning ourselves as the creatures and children of a heavenly Father whose kingdom and will is being made to happen 'on earth as it is in heaven'. This, for me, is the doctrinal starting-point for the gospel, but we have this understanding because it was revealed in and through Christ. So, then, we shall make a beginning.

The nature of God as seen in Christ

The first thing to be clear about is that God *is*. The coming of Christ is, for the Christian, the ultimate proof that humanity is not 'alone in a meaningless universe'. Before us and beyond us there is the One who is what he is. He is the creator of all that is – which in turn invests all that is with significance. Not only is he creator, he is also sustainer. Not only is he sustainer, he is sovereign. He works within the ebb and flow of history to bring about his purposes without violating the genuine freedom of action that is given to us all.

He is judge now. All history bears witness to the fact that those who make themselves into gods through the abuse of power end up as the losers. The wicked are confounded, usually in this life, certainly in the next.

What we see clearly in the example and teaching of Jesus, however, is that the creator, sustainer, king and judge is most nearly and appropriately described in the word 'Father'. The word Jesus used was the trusting, intimate word that would be on the lips of a child – 'Abba'.

To know that in spite of all appearances of randomness and of impersonality in our universe there is a loving heavenly Father is good news indeed. I am not the result of a haphazard cosmic accident. I am meant to be in a world that was meant to be, and meant for me and for all the created order.

And the coming of Christ together with the gift of the Spirit reveals that God wishes to be in a father/child relationship with us. Jesus witnessed to the Father in his teaching, and the Holy Spirit 'testifies with our spirit that we are God's children' (Rom. 8:16). To become a child of God is to become someone who *knowingly* is caught up in God's amazing work within the world – someone who has an awareness (usually imperfect) of God's agenda and who is called to bear witness to it. There are many who – like Cyrus in the Old Testament – are unknowingly serving God's purposes. The privilege for Christians is that they *know* that this is their purpose in life. Purpose in life is a gospel blessing.

The nature of humanity as seen in Christ

While Christ is the supreme revelation of the fact and nature of God, he is also the one who reveals the truth about men and women.

He reveals this truth in two ways. First, in himself he reveals the best that can be said about human beings. We are made in the image of God. We are capable of sacrificial love for others. We are capable of hungering and thirsting for what is right. We are capable of living in constant fellowship with the Father.

At the same time the reaction of people around Jesus to him reveals other aspects of human nature. True goodness is a threat to us. 'Light has come into the world, but men loved darkness instead of light because their deeds were evil,' wrote St John (John 3:19). Whoever met with Jesus was put into a crisis. His presence judged people. They saw humanity as God intended, and it was disturbing. They sensed the presence of God, and the instinctive reaction was to want to say, 'Go away from me, Lord; I am a sinful man!' (Luke 5:8).

The most revealing response to human nature as demonstrated in the total event of Jesus was the crucifixion. People not only rejected the one who came to them as the revealer of God, they set out to destroy him. The crucifixion would not have been possible without a complex of human reactions and behaviour. People with vested interests plotted, those who were religious leaders demonstrated bigotry, those who were political compromisers compromised, people who had opened themselves to evil released their wickedness, those entrusted with the law twisted it, those who were ordered to flog and crucify did not challenge their orders, and hundreds of shallow-thinking, ordinary people went with the tide of opinion and chanted 'crucify'.

What is demonstrated in Christ and in what happened to him is that, while men and women are God's masterpiece

in creation, they are deeply marred by sin. Made to be
God's children, they have naturally tended to be used
by the evil one in opposition to the kingdom. As Jesus
said with a stark finality: 'He who is not with me is
against me' (Matt. 12:30). There seems to be no place
for neutrality in this analysis. Thus we see that human
nature is being judged by Christ and that this judgement
has eternal consequences. The two sides of for and against
are also pictured in the parable of the sheep and the goats
as facing a final and eternal judgement and division (Matt.
25:31–46). To those whose lives (as well as their lips)
revealed a 'for' stance, the judgement is 'Come . . . take
. . . the kingdom prepared for you' (v. 34). For those who
have demonstrated an 'against' stance, the judgement is:
'Depart from me, you who are cursed, into the eternal fire
prepared for the devil and his angels' (v. 41).

Our modern, liberal minds may well find such words
hard to swallow. We will clutch (properly) at the fact
that this is parable and poetic imagery, but it remains
undeniable that Jesus is clearly speaking of ultimate
realities and we have to take his drift seriously. Jesus
is bad news as well as good. Such gospel as we have
is set against the backdrop of humanity under awesome
judgement.

The saving action of God in Christ

'God did not send his Son into the world to condemn
the world, but to save the world through him,' records
St John in John 3:17. To dwell on the themes of judgement and condemnation is to distort what Jesus was all
about. To omit such themes, however, is to make Christ
meaningless.

When our Lord gathered his followers around him to
celebrate the Passover, the meal that celebrated and
re-enacted the saving action of God in Exodus, he rewrote
the script. What emerged was a meal that celebrated
and re-enacted another and greater saving act of God –
the cross.

St Paul was insistent in his teaching that the cross was

at the heart of the gospel. 'I resolved to know nothing while I was with you', he wrote to his friends in Corinth, 'except Jesus Christ and him crucified' (1 Cor. 2:2). To the Galatians he wrote his famous words: 'May I never boast except in the cross of our Lord Jesus Christ, through which the world has been crucified to me, and I to the world' (Gal. 6:14).

The crucifixion marked the height of humanity's rejection of God, but at the same time it demonstrated the way in which God makes forgiveness possible. Many attempts to explain how the cross makes salvation possible end up in crudities, with God somehow being cast in the role of a near-tyrant determined to lash out at somebody and Jesus heroically dashing to the rescue. The New Testament writers do not attempt to spell out the mechanics. What we still find, however, is that the cross was at the heart of God's saving act – this is especially so in Paul's letters. We also see that God is not cast as the outside tyrant, but that he 'was reconciling the world to himself in Christ, not counting men's sins against them' (2 Cor. 5:19).

St Peter recalled the moving prophecy of Isaiah 53 about God's suffering servant who was 'pierced for our transgressions' so that 'by his wounds we are healed'. He wrote: 'He himself bore our sins in his body on the tree, so that we might die to sins and live for righteousness; by his wounds you have been healed' (1 Pet. 2:24).

What is important about the atonement is that it has happened in Christ. It is much less important to be able to explain it exactly. However, the saving act of God, while focused on the cross, should not be limited to it. The whole 'event' of Jesus from birth to resurrection and ascension is part of God's great saving act. It was the resurrection that changed the Jesus story from a humanity-centred tragedy to a God-centred triumph. It 'declared with power' that Jesus was Son of God (Rom. 1:4). The first Christians would never have concluded as they did about Christ and the cross had it not been for the resurrection – a resurrection that they witnessed and were certain was genuine because of 'many convincing proofs' (Acts 1:3).

Today, as we contemplate the life, death and resurrection of Jesus, we find ourselves looking at another world – another and more important level of reality – breaking into our own. For the space of a few years the king and the kingdom of God broke into the muddy affairs of our own regimes. The Jesus story opens our eyes to see reality as it truly is. We develop an understanding of ourselves as well as God. We catch a vision for how we should live and where we are going. And as the New Testament writers describe what we call the ascension, the message to all who will follow is: 'Watch this space.' There is more to come for the story of the planet, and there is eternally more to come for all who are 'for' Jesus.

The nature of this age

The new Christian who takes sides with Jesus and who sets out to 'walk in the Spirit' will find 'joy and peace' in believing (Rom. 15:13), but will also experience tension upon tension. There is the internal tug-of-war between the 'old nature' dominated by self-centred concerns and the 'new nature' opening up to the Spirit of God. There is the tension of human mortality in which our hope of eternal life still has to reckon with our experience of growing older and frailer as we approach physical death. There is the tension of trying to live as those who are 'for' Christ in a world that both wittingly and unwittingly is caught up in the dynamics of being 'against' him. There is also the mysterious reality of finding ourselves caught up in the kingdom of light as it engages with the kingdom of darkness. St Paul wrote: 'our struggle is not against flesh and blood, but against the rulers, against the authorities, against the powers of this dark world and against the spiritual forces of evil in the heavenly realms' (Eph. 6:12).

To respond to the story of Jesus is to be caught up in it and to enter, or at least touch parts of, the levels of reality in which God works. This is what it means to be a new person in Christ. It is good news, but it is no picnic. Unless we help seekers to understand the truth about the age in which we live, we are preaching a false gospel. When, however, people learn that the kingdom of God which broke out in and around Jesus also breaks into our world in and around those who seek to follow him (and beyond them in the purposes of God), then they will see that there is good news indeed in Christ. Further, all that we experience in these fragmentary ways in the present will finally come in fullness when God's will is done 'on earth as it is in heaven'.

Conclusion

Evangelism and doctrine are inseparable. The gospel event is the raw material from which all central Christian doctrines are developed. Evangelism is the communication of the story, and the implications, of the Jesus event. While many may find themselves drawn towards belief and commitment through the effect of warm human relationships, it is through a 'renewing of the mind' (Rom. 12:2) that conversion becomes a reality. That renewal requires a grasp of the right understandings – and thus we are talking about doctrine.

But the biggest hold-up to evangelism rests in the set of understandings that many have, not about the content of the gospel, but about the nature of the church.

If we believe the church is meant to be no more than a club for believers, or even to be *fully* described as a 'congregation of faithful men, in the which the pure Word of God is preached, and the Sacraments be duly administered' (Article 19), then we run the risk of having an understanding of 'church' to which evangelism is almost totally alien. It is here that we need to see the church in terms of the people of God called to declare his name and his worthiness to the world at large. To say this, however, is to make a doctrinal statement.

Questions for discussion

1. In what ways does a wrong understanding of the church hinder evangelism?

2. How do we evangelise in the light of the fact that most conversions are gradual?
3. Is the author's claim justified that the digest of the gospel on pp. 70–1 is too man-centred? If so, what is the problem?
4. If doctrine is of greatest importance at the nurture stage, what should evangelists talk about?

For further reading

William Abraham, *The Logic of Evangelism* (London: Hodder & Stoughton, 1989)

Peter Ball, *Adult Believing* (London: Mowbrays, 1988)

Michael Marshall, *The Gospel Connection* (London: Darton, Longman & Todd, 1991)

Lesslie Newbigin, *Truth to Tell* (London: SPCK, 1991)

Donald Posterski, *Reinventing Evangelism* (Downers Grove, IL.: IVP, 1989)

Stephen Sykes, 'An Anglican Theology of Evangelism', *Theology* 94 (November–December, 1991), pp. 405–14

Gavin Reid is Bishop of Maidstone in the Diocese of Canterbury. He was Consultant Missioner with the Church Pastoral Aid Society (CPAS) and a member of General Synod, and served on its Board of Mission. After six years in parochial ministry and eight years in religious publishing, he concentrated on strategic evangelistic ministry. In the 1980s he was twice seconded by the CPAS to direct missions in the UK for Dr Billy Graham. In 1991 he was installed as a 'Six Preacher' in Canterbury Cathedral.

5

Doctrine and Worship

Colin Buchanan

Introduction: The origins of today's trinitarianism

It has become my habit to enquire of clergy, ordinands, lay leaders and adult confirmation candidates why they are trinitarians. They usually find the question disconcerting, but patient persistence starts to yield a clear picture. Today's believers, if they are trinitarian at all, are so because they recite creeds, encounter the baptismal formula, say 'The Grace' together, and sing three-verse hymns, addressed verse by verse to each of the three persons of the Trinity. The cumulative effect of these interlocking items is to convince worshippers at the very least that the Christian doctrine of God is that he is to be understood in a trinitarian way – while at most it convinces the individual worshipper that she or he should so believe and trust in God for herself or himself.

But without these materials, how would a believer in Jesus Christ know how to think about God? Reading the Bible on one's own or in a small group *might* bring an enquirer near to the answer, but the actual paradoxes in the unity of the Godhead and the threeness of the 'persons' are such as to baffle people enquiring on their own. Indeed, they are more likely to fall into heresy, as the sole escape from the wildly impossible statement – that which defines the Trinity – to which the biblical wisps of evidence would seem to be driving them.

Historically, of course, it took till 451, and more than a century of hot controversy, before the church reached anything like a settled mind on the issue. It is therefore arguable that any individual who tries to reason the matter out by herself or himself is very likely either to get it wrong if the quest is completed within one lifetime, or alternatively never to get it done at all, if the quest is allowed to run to its proper length. The individual must be rare indeed who, with a *tabula rasa* of a mind, labours over an open Bible, and nothing but a Bible, from which to learn the truth of God, but nevertheless comes up with an orthodox doctrine of the Trinity. We may go further, and postulate that either the person does not exist and never has done, or, if such an individual does once in a millennium come up with the truth, then that doctrine is as likely to be a freak result, a coincidence, or the outcome of a combination of mutually cancelling errors.

We do not abate one inch from the position that all that needs to be known of God is to be found in scripture. We still affirm that the scripture is in broad terms transparent and teaches God's truth. But to ask our lone individual to function without outside assistance from others around him or her in the present, or from commentators or theologians from the past – that is a self-defeating programme. If we go further and expect that lone individual to discern the raw materials of Christian doctrine in the scriptures, to draw together the different materials into a single formulated whole, to bombard that formulation with every kind of difficulty and objection, to adjust the formulation to meet the difficulties, and then smilingly to present the upshot as rounded and tested statements of Christian doctrine (as, e.g., in the case of the Trinity) – then that is to go too far. We cheerfully conclude that God's provision of an open Bible was not intended to fulfil that function, and we are driven back to allocating great value to the debates of Christian history and the importance of received traditional formulations. Such formulations are still open to revision in the light of scripture, but the valuing of them is a starting-point in seeing the role of traditional worship materials in the inculcation and preservation of the central doctrines of the faith.

We may add a further quirk. When the doctrine *was* under debate in the fourth and fifth centuries, it was resolved not only by comparing scripture with scripture, but also by the church reflecting on *how it already worshipped*. Of course there was a theoretical possibility that previous worship was incorrect, but the general assumption in the early church was that the inherited ways of worship had (at the very least) a strong *prima facie* case for being a measure of orthodoxy. Thus a church which worshipped Christ as God could not avoid a credal affirmation that he *is* God – and yet not in such a way as to involve there being two or more gods.

So we propound a dynamic in the conveying of doctrine – a conveying well illustrated in the case of that difficult but vital formulation, the Trinity – from one generation to the next:

- Doctrine is revealed in holy scripture.
- It is enshrined in historic ways of worship.
- It is crystallised and formulated under pressure of controversy, when the scripture and ways of worship are in dialogue.
- This crystallisation reinforces the role of doctrine in the ways of worship, as thereafter that doctrine emerges in worship not simply by accident, but by careful design.
- Nevertheless the formulations are always up for judgement by the supreme authority in matters of faith and doctrine – scripture itself – and they are to be tested anew by scripture in each new generation.
- The unsophisticated – perhaps almost all the church – in fact learn their doctrine from inherited (and often imposed) ways of worship. (The sophisticated

can of course test for themselves the exactness of the formulations by recourse to the full text of the scripture, but this is a discipline beyond the reach of most of the church for virtually the whole of history.)

We might add to this account that, even in unsophisticated people and unlettered periods of history, forms of worship do not stand quite alone as conveying the word of God from one generation to the next. There are also credal, confessional, and catechetical forms. Even these find their ways into the language of worship, so that a constant mutual dialogue has been observed down history. And ways of worship should not be confined too closely to verbal texts – the sheer arrangement of a congregation in a place of worship, the very location of the leaders of the assembly, and the position of, say, a communion table in relation to the congregation, will also be silently eloquent about our doctrine of the church and sacraments. Anything I say hereafter about the role of doctrine in worship should be reckoned to include these non-verbal statements, for all that the normal revelation of God is by word, and that the norm of the inclusion of God's revelation in our worship events is by word also. The word is primary, and sacraments, music, buildings, furnishings, and art underline and reinforce (or sometimes contradict and weaken) what is handed on in word. The doctrine imparted thereby is not mediated solely by word, but it is always under judgement from the norms which are verbal.

Doctrine is always in principle doxological*

Scripture and liturgy differ, of course, in their authority. The scripture is primary and non-negotiable, while liturgy is derivative, more flexible and more contingent. But they also differ in their form. Scripture involves a plethora of

*(i.e., such that it can be expressed in worship)

styles, written for a multitude of purposes. The Gospels include biography, apologetics, ethics, soteriology, homiletics, etc. The Epistles include autobiography, polemics about orthodoxy, *euchology* (i.e., ground rules for prayer), pastoralia, etc. Worship *motifs* run through these writings and 'telling the Christian story' is part of the task of worship. History itself comes into the Gospels and Acts, into the personal background to Paul's letters, into references to Jesus having come in the flesh to be crucified and to be raised from the dead, and into every reference to how God has already been at work in the lives of Paul's (or Peter's or John's) readers.

So there is a vast overlap of materials, or at least a heavy dependence of forms of worship upon the text of scripture. This in turn means that those forms become the vehicle for conveying the knowledge of the word of God (in whatever flexible form) from one generation to another. And the understanding of scripture is in turn largely influenced by the current experience and context of the church which is reading scripture – and that current experience and context includes at a very deep level the experience of worship. How the church worships becomes how it understands God's truth.

But scripture is still supreme

One of the major differences between the early centuries of the church and the present day lies in the availability of the scriptures. We are used to a dozen or more translations being ready to hand; we are used to a version of some sort being in every home; we can hand out matching versions with identical page numbers to a confirmation class or a Bible study group. The texts are simply *there*.

But that was not so in the early centuries. Printing was unknown, and texts were rare and precious. Indeed the word of God was thought to be somehow embodied in the person of the bishop, and his role was to teach. As he also presided over worship, it was understood that the two were in line with each other, and mutually interpreting.

The only danger sign from our point of view was that forms of worship, having developed unselfconsciously over the generations, began to assume an autonomy which was not open to question. The liturgical tradition had a 'givenness' comparable to that of the scripture. No worshipping community would have dreamed in the early centuries of criticising, let alone deliberately reforming, the liturgical uses which they themselves had inherited. Certainly church leaders (and even pilgrims) would know that traditions varied from one place to another. Certainly bright ideas from one place might, it seems, occasionally get slipped into the rites of another. But the general principle was that the forms of worship reflected and embodied the truths of God beyond argument, and they should therefore be always expounded in an orthodox sense, and never be called in question.

From our point of view, not every primitive text is quite so univocally orthodox, and thus the exposition could have a somewhat forced character to it. A small instance: I once published (in my Grove Books' capacity) a most stimulating and delightful monograph by Rowan Williams, *Eucharistic Sacrifice – the Roots of a Metaphor*, and was struck by a quotation from a sermon of Ephrem the Syrian (though it is easily paralleled elsewhere in ancient Christian authors).[1] Ephrem expounds Simeon's greeting of the infant Christ in the temple as an offering of him to God, and then explores deeper significances of that oblation. But the underlying point is that 'offering Christ' is in some way part of his pattern of thought and speech – and this is almost certainly due to the oblationary emphases in his weekly eucharistic rite. As a matter of fact, the Bible presents some difficulties for an idea expressed in this way, and so Ephrem has to go on to re-explain it. He thus (almost without reflection) reconciles Bible and liturgical text – but what he cannot do, which is what the Reformers later did, is to challenge the contingent form of the liturgy from the surer ground of the Bible.

This in turn puts some constraints upon the use of primitive forms made by the English Reformers – and points to some constraints which should be upon us today. The Reformers admittedly spoke of seeking out the uses of the early church, and, although they had a somewhat smaller range of primitive texts and materials than are available to us today, they were by no means lacking in scholarship. Yet, in the last analysis, they were only ransacking the early centuries for good precedents for changes that they wished in fact to make on other (i.e., biblical) grounds – or were seeking materials to demonstrate polemically that Rome did not now stand where the early church had stood. The early authors were themselves not autonomous in the things of God, and, though they might well at times be bearers of God's truth, that was a matter for testing by scripture, not for mere assertion. Indeed, it might well be argued that the Church of England formally crossed a very significant line when Cranmer's Article VII of 1553 (Article VIII of 1571) declared that the three Creeds ' . . . ought thoroughly to be received [and believed, 1571]: *for they may be proved by most certain warrants of holy Scripture*' (italics mine). Catholic grounds for receiving the Creeds might have been that they had the force of General Councils behind them, or that they had always and everywhere and by everyone been believed and recited – but both those grounds are ignored, the inherited texts are resubmitted to the test of scripture, and they are declared orthodox *on scriptural grounds*.

From this the formal principle emerges that scripture is 'supreme' over all traditions, including traditions of worship. This was a principle well down the list in the logical chain I set out on pages 81–2 above. It is first well focused in the Reformation controversies. And, if it is formally stated in the Thirty-nine Articles, it is constantly illustrated from the very earliest progress of the Reformation. It is, for instance, hardly a coincidence that one of the earliest changes in almost every part of Europe where the Reformation came was the restoration of the eucharistic cup to the laity. The contrast was stark and clear – the inherited tradition of worship was that the bread alone was given to the people (a pattern which spread quite fast in the wake of the decree of the Fourth Lateran Council in 1215 enforcing the doctrine of transubstantiation): but when people could read the scriptures they found that at the last supper Jesus had not only said, 'Drink this . . . ', but had even added (for the cup alone) as though in a particularly prescient way: ' . . . all of you'. The issue presented itself once the Bible was read, and it pushed people into one of two camps – either the worship tradition was autonomous (in which case it had to be viewed as compatible with the Bible at whatever cost in logic, perspicuity or common sense – and there would be no excuse for altering it), or it was subject to judgement by the Bible (in which case it could be and should be altered). Men and women fell into two camps as they adopted one of two mutually exclusive principles.

To summarise: we discover that the right expectation is that the texts of worship should foster and sustain the word of God in euchological (and doxological) form[2] and should thus pass them from one generation to the next; and the faith is regularly learned, and learned aright, by worshippers benefiting from this principle. However, the tradition may digress from the truth or become fossilised, and it is then up for judgement in the light of scripture. So the church has a constant duty to review its forms of worship, both treasuring its traditions on the one hand, and being ready to alter whatever is not true to scripture on the other.

Worship is more than a correct verbal statement of truth

Once the above principles are clear, it is timely to issue a warning. Worship is not exhaustively defined by its correct reproduction of doctrinal orthodoxy. Ideally, worship is a function of people, not programmes; it stems from the heart as well as from the mind; it bonds and unites those who engage together in it; it is the point of corporate meeting with God and building up of God's people in love;

it is the point of earnest repentance, praise and petition; it is the point where God's word is proclaimed (usually in an unprogrammed way); and it is the point where sharing together at the Lord's table has values, meanings and obligations running far beyond what is formally expressed in words. As with preaching, so with every other element of worship – there is a strong responsibility resting upon the leader to plan the scriptural and doctrinal content as carefully as possible, but to look to God to do more than we can ask or think even through our plans.

Worship may also include (like sermons!) a greater or lesser degree of extemporary elements. A baptism rite may include personal testimony; prayers should often be not only related to topical needs, but should also in many situations be contributed on the spot by many worshippers. The doctrinal content of such contributions may be low (or even occasionally heretical), but their enriching of liturgy is beyond all doubt. They do, however, emphasise the need for a responsible doctrinal framework (usually indeed 'the tradition') to support the contemporary elements. The Christian story is to be told and retold as the context of extemporary prayer and informal praise.

So Christian worship may include more than correct verbalisation of truth – but it must not include less. The freer the extemporary parts are, the more secure must the doctrinal framework be. That does not, of course, have to be an inflexible rubric for every single act of corporate worship – we are right to assume some reasonable continuity of our congregations from week to week, and to plan both framework and freedom to provide the right integration of them over a considerable period of time. Indeed, it might well be argued that the Christian year provides exactly that period of time – and that the existence of fixed foci of the year at Christmas, Easter and Pentecost gives a strengthening to the doctrinal framework, while leaving great scope for 'ordinary' seasons to exhibit less concentrated attention on the incarnation, the atonement and resurrection, and the coming of the Spirit. Instead, the low seasons can be employed more opportunistically for themes and even syllabuses which are precipitated more by the worshippers' known needs and gaps and less by our convictions about God's own priorities. Of course those who attend only at harvest will hardly hear much about the cross (except from the determined preacher prepared to exploit John 12:24 for soteriological purposes!). But we cannot pour the whole of Christian doctrine into any one event, and the Christian year provides in a serene and objective way that vital framework of true belief over its period of time. Any arbitrary selectivity about themes should then become self-correcting, as the round of the year puts into the forms of worship the great central doctrinal concerns of the church.

The reforming principle at work in the Reformation

For those of us who are Anglicans, it is worth spelling out more fully how this principle of the supremacy of scripture worked through into our forms of worship in the Reformation period. We may almost spell it out in a logical chain of procedure:

1. The existing liturgical rites continued when Henry separated from Rome. They were 'the tradition' and they were not lightly to be attacked or altered.

2. When the thoroughgoing doctrinal reformation came about in Edward VI's reign (1547–53), the existing Latin rites remained lawful, even while their successors were being planned. Small inroads were made, such as first the requirement to read the Epistle and Gospel in English (1547), and then the insertion of the English-language *The Order of the Communion* into the mass, with a view to distributing both elements to the people, with some vernacular devotions first (1548). The very minor character of these changes was an affirmation that the tradition was being respected, and, although it would be duly reformed, this would not be by wholesale abolition and the creating of wholly new forms overnight. The scriptures *were* judging the texts, and reform *would* come, but the tradition was being allowed its interim status.

and its worship forms will tell you. We may be less confessing and rather nearer to witnessing than in the sixteenth and seventeenth centuries, but the concept that our doctrinal stance shines through our liturgical forms is no less present.

Some modern issues

If we take the view set out above, we may well conclude that liturgy, in so far as we can write down, or put on record, with what words and actions people worshipped in different ages, is actually a form of historical theology. It expresses doctrine and presents a church's doctrinal stance. In worship it moves and forms the people who use it (and it may be presumed to be received benevolently by God himself also): out of worship it gives formal continuity to the faith of a church which itself has an *ontology* (formal existence) even when it is not actually meeting.

Thus it was worship forms which were under review when the papal encyclical *Apostolicae Curae* of 1896 condemned Anglican orders. What were orders *for*? Why, to provide a valid priesthood. Why did we want a valid priesthood? To secure a true eucharistic sacrifice offered by a truly sacrificing priesthood? How should we know that any eucharist was meant to be an offering of the eucharistic sacrifice? Why, by inspecting the text. The Pope duly inspected the eucharistic rites of 1552 and 1662, and concluded that any presbyters ordained to preside at such rites *could* not have been expected to do what the Catholic Church does at the eucharist, and thus, by argument backwards from the liturgy, the Anglican presbyterate was declared no true priesthood. Irrespective of whether the Pope's conclusion was or was not right on his own terms, the interest for us this minute is that the doctrine of the ministry was being settled on the basis of the eucharistic liturgy – and its historical development in Anglicanism. Similarly, when the Anglican Archbishops replied in 1897, asserting the validity of Anglican ordinations from the sixteenth century onwards, they replied in terms of the ordination rites and eucharistic rites. In my view they got it wrong (for they tried to find a eucharistic sacrifice in the 1662 rite which was drafted to exclude it). But they were handling the right materials – for liturgical uses do give birth to doctrine, and it would have been useless to have replied to the Pope without reference to Anglican liturgical rites.

I go back to *Apostolicae Curae* partly because I cherish a slight niggle about a more recent comparison of eucharistic doctrine in the two churches. The first Anglican/Roman Catholic International Commission concluded in September 1971 an agreement on the eucharist, finally published on 31 December 1971.[5] That first common statement has had great currency over the last twenty years; despite some strains in handling its most sensitive points, it has won wide acclaim; and broadly it has been backed by Anglicans of every school, and only marginally queried, very recently, by Rome itself. But irrespective of its merits as a formal accord on eucharistic doctrine, the complaint I am making is that the agreement had a dogmatic character *unrelated to the actual official liturgical texts of both churches*. It is indeed arguable that the two sides agreed with each other but had no agreement with their own texts. Certainly the Anglican texts of the period up to 1971 exhibited a very large range of doctrinal emphases (not all of which would have readily fitted with the agreement); while on the Roman Catholic side the new post-Vatican II eucharistic prayers – in so many ways a great advance on their predecessors – still expressed doctrines of eucharistic sacrifice which went far beyond the agreed statement, and could hardly be squared with it.

Conservative liturgy and liberal theologians?

I now want to open up a totally different area of doctrine and liturgy. When I first joined the Liturgical Commission in September 1964, Anthony Hanson (who was then the Church of Ireland observer) took me aside and told me not to worry about high church tendencies, but rather to be on the alert for the 'South Bank' (this was in the early days after the publication of *Honest to God*[6]). We did at the time have both the Bishop and the Provost of Southwark on the Commission, but neither was going to commit doctrinal enormities. Indeed, my conservative self found the Commission reasonably comforting – the deep sense that, even when being creative, you are running within a doctrinal tradition is reassuring, and there was, as far as I could see at the time, no mind (whether from inside or from outside the Commission) to challenge the tradition. The Commission in particular was not doctrinally iconoclastic. At least, it was not until one day, when . . .

It happened in a symposium produced to accompany Series 3 Communion, the rite which first addressed God as 'you' and was authorised as an alternative service from February 1973. The symposium was edited by Ronald Jasper, was entitled *The Eucharist Today: Studies on Series 3*, and was published in 1974. The last contribution in this was by Leslie Houlden, a member of the Commission, and a somewhat 'liberal' theologian. His chapter, dubbed 'Liturgy and her Companions: A Theological Appraisal', protested at the credal conservatism of the eucharistic rite (and indeed of all the Commission's work) in the following terms:

If you dig, you find an astonishing phenomenon. You discover that the principles of liturgy have become disciplines in their own right, quite apart from other aspects of Christian thought. It is a fact that is worth contemplating, for it is surely quite new in Christian life, that liturgy can be constructed without significant reference to the total theological scene and seeing itself as an independent skill . . .

Demythologizing, whether mild or severe, may indeed lead to an impoverishment of imagery. It can equally lead to a restoration of a sense of the living God by removing the opiate of an obsolete story . . . [The eucharistic Preface] speaks of alleged 'events' of the

distant past, while admittedly drawing some attention
to their lasting effect. God, ages ago, created, gave
liberation from sin, and brought into being a people
. . . however much weight we place on the life and death
of Jesus, the faithful believer will not be content to see
'redemption' as tied exclusively to those events . . . the
old purely historical-cum-theological approach persists
– in obedience to liturgical tradition, and, behind that,
to the canonizing of a particular way of regarding the
witness of Scripture.

    . . . we praise God for creation through Jesus, his
living Word. We appeal thereby to a biblical and
patristic concept, that of Christ as the pre-existent
Logos . . .

    But quite apart from cases of extreme difficulty such
as this . . . is continued biblical allusion necessarily
the right way to make satisfactory modern liturgy?
May twentieth century Christians not pray in words
of their own?[7]

This chapter of Leslie Houlden's has been the subject
of much comment, and has almost become a point of
reference as a *locus classicus*. He has himself reprinted
it once. I had a go at meeting his position head-on in my
chapter 'The Liturgist in the Church' in a pre-Lambeth
symposium of 1988, *The Trial of Faith*.[8] As I have since
continued to hear the idea around that somehow Houlden
has thrown down a gauntlet none dare pick up, I prefer
to think that my chapter has not been read (rather than,
having been read, it has been discarded as useless). I
therefore venture to repeat the headings of my reply. In
summary, they come out thus:

1. Liturgy stands close to scripture, and to the creeds.
When the *creeds* are rewritten to exclude (say) the creation, or the life, death and resurrection of Jesus Christ,
then liturgy can take the same steps (though we would not
have much left). If demythologising is a proper discipline,
then it must come into force *after* the crossing of the Red
Sea has taken its place in liturgy, not before. The 'story'

has its place in creed and liturgy and means there no more or less than in the scripture.

2. If we allow the theologians this demythologisation, where does it end? Is the empty tomb 'myth'? Is all hymnody about Jesus rising from the dead to be 'demythologised', so that we do not say he 'rose' but only that he survived (or whatever)?

3. What alternative programme of liturgy-writing is on offer? Houlden writes of imagery as 'riotous and exciting as possible', which sounds wonderful (though, we have to remember, neither the riot nor the excitement can be generated from scripture). Indeed, what are these 'words of their own' with which twentieth-century Christians are to pray?

4. We might, of course, also throw the issue back to the theologians. Are they all of this Houlden school? Would all of them deplore scriptural imagery as a way of praying today? Indeed, should scripture itself be read in liturgy, if it can only mislead and needs replacing? Can the average layperson be trusted to read or hear the scriptures (let alone mark and inwardly digest them)? Where does the Houlden thesis take us as pastors?

Perhaps the fleeting whims of theological schools *need* the relative stability of scriptural liturgy to undergird their volatility. And while it is clear that ceremonies and rituals of a secular character can be devised (or can even arise through the corruption of Christian ceremonies), if the ceremonies we value are in fact to *be* Christian, then the Christian story will run through them. A health-giving spiral is then set up – our forms of worship will whet our doctrinal appetites, and our scriptural studies will invade our forms of worship. If, as the people of God, we are 'not to live by bread alone, but by every word that proceeds from the mouth of God'; and if a community lives by its communal activities – i.e. by its liturgical life, then it is clear that the word of God and the patterns of our worship must interact upon each other for their communal life to be life in God. Christian doctrine should conserve that word of God, depending not only upon the given data of scripture, but also upon the living expression of the word in worship. And the word of God, thus conserved, should in turn both charter and empower, but equally monitor and restrain, the ways in which we worship. If a health-giving cycle is established, then our worship of God in Christ not only brings glory to God, but, through the penetration of God's truth into our lives, also becomes food to the inner hunger, drink to the thirsty soul.

Questions for discussion

1. How did *you* learn Christian doctrine (e.g., the doctrine of the Trinity), and how do you know you have got it right?
2. What impact on your understanding of the Christian faith has come from items in public worship, such as, e.g., (a) sermons, (b) hymns, (c) public reading of scripture, (d) prayers, (e) extemporary or informal contributions?
3. What do you learn about the beliefs of other denominations from their ways of worship?

For further reading

Baptism, Eucharist and Ministry (The Lima Text), World Council of Churches Faith and Order Paper III (Geneva: WCC, 1982)

Colin Buchanan, 'The Liturgist in the Church', in Peter Eaton (ed.), *The Trial of Faith* (London: Churchman, 1988), pp. 143–61

Stephen Sykes, *The Integrity of Anglicanism* (London: Mowbray, 1978)

Geoffrey Wainwright, *Doxology: Systematic Theology – The Praise of God in Worship, Doctrine and Life* (London: Epworth Press, 1980), the major (encyclopaedic) work

Colin Buchanan was ordained in 1961, and, after one curacy, joined the staff of the London College of Divinity (which is now St John's Nottingham) in 1964, to teach Christian worship. At the same time he became a member of the Liturgical Commission, and served on it till 1986, in which time all the liturgical revision which lies behind and in the ASB was completed. From 1970 (when the College went to Nottingham) to 1985 he was also on the General Synod. In 1979 he became Principal of St John's College. In 1985 he became Bishop of Aston, and, on resigning from that office in 1989, he became an assistant bishop in the diocese of Rochester, and is currently vicar of St Mark's Church, Gillingham. He is the original founder and now manager of Grove Books, the editor of *News of Liturgy*, and the author of many books. He was a member of the Doctrine Commission from 1986 to 1991.

6

Doctrine and Spirituality

Vera Sinton

'Spirituality' has become a popular buzz-word, and not just among religious believers. The notion of a spiritual dimension to human life is being used much more widely than a decade ago. Then post-war rationalism was at its peak. In schools and colleges or in the media there was a confident assumption that all knowledge comes to us by seeing, hearing, feeling, touching, smelling. Truth comes from sense data processed in the logical reasoning capacity of the brain. In the climate of hard-nosed management of the early 1980s, rationalism linked hands with science, technology and bureaucratic efficiency to establish a public domain where decisions are based on 'facts'. 'Values' were relegated to the private sector of leisure, entertainment and family life. Now, in the supposedly caring 1990s, some of the personal values are creeping back into the public realm, clothing themselves furtively as 'facts'.

The new secular spirituality

Some big institutions and businesses are paying attention to their human resources and emphasising the personal values that make an impact on people. Techniques that develop character and aid self-knowledge are being explored in the growing industry of management and personnel training. In one sense there is nothing new about that. Twentieth-century psychology has often been applied to personnel training and human development. To see what is significant we have to notice where the model of what is an ideal person is changing. Rational secularism thrives on a humanist ideal of a thoroughly independent, healthy, self-confident individual, body and mind, exploring, interpreting and acting in a self-contained material world. Now, in our post-modern world, a model popular with the semi-religious 'New Age' movement is coming to the fore.

The idea gaining ground is that at the centre of a human being is a 'self' (soul or psyche) which has the ability to connect with a higher self, often described as 'transpersonal'. A person can tune into a source of power by a form of communication that is above and beyond the intellect and the five senses. An important step, according to this thinking, is that you learn how to become 'centred'. You start by making contact with your feelings of the present moment and bringing them into tune with your thinking. Then you gradually reduce the clutter and activity of your mind to a point of inner stillness where the well-spring of the higher self is to be found. Feelings have a biological component as well as a mental one. So posture, physical relaxation, breathing are seen as important. Focusing your attention on the view or a work of art or a natural object, doing mental exercises which guide the imagination, or reciting familiar words of liturgy or verse, all these are seen as maps or walking sticks on the journey towards inner attentiveness and contemplation.

During a recent sabbatical, I attended a university-run extension course in human relations which had a programme remarkably similar in structure to a small Christian conference. There were talks and sharing, meditations and testimonies, trust exercises and games. When finally we stood in a circle, holding hands, and affirmed each other with eye contact, only the words of the Grace were missing.

The fact is that none of these components is new. A whole range of techniques for settling into personal meditation or for creating a sense of fellowship in a group have been used down the centuries by Christians in worship or at prayer. They are part of a wider set of techniques drawn on by the members of pagan or occult sects as well as by the adherents of the major world religions. The fact that there is common ground should not surprise us, but Christians have always been alert to dangers and differences as well as areas of overlap. Not every numinous feeling or experience of transcendent power is going to be wholesome in the life of the believer. There are practices which squander human energy, lead to destructive emotions or distort the mind's grasp of truth and reality.

The language of centring and of self may contain some new turns of phrase, but it has a strong family likeness to ancient Eastern mysticism. The new element in 'New Age' thinking is the way it rubs shoulders with modern Western materialism. You can speak the language of the new spirituality, and practise meditation and spiritual growth while remaining distinctly agnostic about the power behind the experience. Television producers love to leave the truth question tantalisingly open in dramas and documentaries about the paranormal. Are there transpersonal forces beyond our categories of explanation? Or will they all soon be explained in some new unified scientific understanding of energy waves, superstrings or whatever?

The New Age movement is parallel with Buddhism in teaching meditation and prayer while remaining agnostic about the existence of God. It does not share the Eastern mystics' condemnation of wealth and desire. Centring and getting in touch with the higher self is more likely to be seen as a recipe for powerful and successful living in a technological world. The new spirituality encourages its adherents to assert a large measure of control over their own destinies. In the process they may draw on any and every religion and practice; whatever works. There need be no uncomfortable clash with other religions and beliefs. Are we not all people on the way, journeying towards the love of God, whoever or whatever God may turn out to be? It is the answer to that question which is increasingly confusing and dividing Christian people today.

Christian spirituality: the traditional metaphors

The Christian traditions of spirituality revolve around a triangle whose three points are:

- God who is Spirit, immortal, invisible, other than us.
- The inner consciousness of the individual person, I-myself, thinking, feeling, deciding, worshipping, praying.
- The external world of human beings, they or we, relating to one another in a created physical environment.

One starting-place is to see Christian spirituality as knowing God, loving and being loved by God, having a relationship with him. An alternative approach is to say that Christian spirituality is about life, 'the outworking of our Christian life from becoming a Christian to death or Christ's return' (Phil. 2:12–13).[1] Both of these approaches contain key metaphors from basic human experience. The first is the analogy of intimate human relationships, getting to know a parent or friend, a colleague or a lover. The second is a comparison with biological life and growth. A seed germinates or a creature is born. There is an initial rapid transformation followed by the process of growth which is gradual and variable. Each specimen within a species has recognisable characteristics of its species but its combination of shape and size, health, fruitfulness and beauty are unique.

The biblical writers and Christian spiritual writers down the centuries make extensive use of these complementary ideas of knowing and growing. The first puts the spotlight on God, the one we seek and thirst for, hungry to hear his voice and see his face. The second makes us the focus of attention, yet it also emphasises our dependence. Control does not lie with us. 'Who of you by worrying can add a single cubit to his height?' (Matt. 6:27). We grow spiritually as the Spirit of God flows in us and through us. In New Testament writings, especially those of Paul and John, there are times when it is notoriously difficult for the translators to decide whether to use spirit or Spirit to translate the Greek term '*pneuma*' (e.g., John 4:24; 1 Cor. 14:15). Perhaps the apostolic writers enjoyed the ambiguity of such sentences. What is spiritual about me is not a discrete part of me labelled 'spirit', but my whole person infused with the Spirit of God.

Relationship with God or growing into maturity: these by no means exhaust the Christian metaphors for spirituality. Another significant pair occur in the language of travelling and fighting. The Old Testament story devotes much space to the journey of the people of God towards the land of promise. Jesus describes his disciples as those on the narrow way which leads to life. The earliest label for the Christian religion was 'the Way' (Acts 9:2). Journeying is an immensely popular concept in recent literature on spirituality, both Christian and also the new secular variety. Here we see some of the tension between the inner focus and the external one, mentioned above. Is the journey which we are on an inward journey away from the distractions and concerns of the external world, towards what is 'purely spiritual'? Or is it a pilgrimage side by side with one another into and through the world?

After the exodus and entry into the land, the Old Testament emphasis changes to the battle to defend it against hostile forces who challenge the sovereign reign of the Lord. New Testament spirituality makes strong use of the language of warfare against demons and the devil and corporate human structures.

So knowing and growing, going or overcoming: all of these are active metaphors. How important, then, is a relatively static deposit of Christian doctrine in the dynamics of the spiritual life?

Spirituality as knowing God

For many writers a key starting-point for Christian spirituality is the well-known sentence from Christ's high priestly prayer in John 17:3, 'This is eternal life: that they may know you, the only true God, and Jesus Christ, whom you have sent.' The context is Jesus at prayer between the final supper when he instituted the Holy Communion and his crucifixion from which that meal takes its meaning. His longing is that his flock should know God. Consider three implications of the verse.

First, it is to know 'the only true God'. There is a duality; there is such a thing as falsehood. There are diverse alternatives. Some things are to be rejected. Christian spirituality is a thirst for, a search for the unique and genuine God.

Second, it hinges on knowing Jesus. At a specific point in human history God has been revealed through a man, Jesus the Son who became a servant and was sent on a rescue mission. God is not an uninvolved inventor, nor is he an impersonal force. God is personal, and is personally involved in the pain of the world he made and loves.

Third, it embraces life. Eternal life in John's Gospel is not a shadowy, uncharted future existence. It includes all that is real, valuable, exuberant and loving in human experience here and now. Then it expands its horizon in the confident hope that this is just a finite fragment of what life in relationship with God for eternity will be like. Knowing God is not something to be put in a separate box labelled 'spiritual' which is divorced from the normal process of living. For beginners in the spiritual life, getting to know God may seem to be primarily about the inner life of prayer, but spirituality is always a wider concept. It embraces life to the full.

The spiritual life is dynamic because it is a movement in the direction of eliminating what is false and harmful and coming to a genuine relationship of knowing the true God. Progress in this coincides with experiencing a quality of living which is good in its own right but only a small advance on what is to come in the future. It is inextricably bound up with the historical life, death and resurrection of Jesus Christ.

Doctrine as knowing about God

If we use this approach, and see spirituality as knowing God, with its complementary aspect of growing in life, doctrine takes its place as knowing about God.

Consider the comparison with human relationships. When two people are in the early stages of getting to know each other they tend to talk a great deal and feel uncomfortable with silence. They long for information and bombard the other person with direct or indirect questions. What is he like? What has she done? What choices is this person likely to make? What values does he cherish? Each of us has our own framework of interests into which we are fitting the messages received. One person may develop a very deep and important friendship with another without knowing whether her parents are still alive or if she has a sister. Someone else may consider this information essential to any claim to 'know' her. We vary in what we take note of, but the differences are variations on a set of themes we share with others in our culture.

The categories we are exploring are mainly ones we have learned. On the whole our memories do not stretch back to the time when we were infants and encountered a visitor as a mass of impressions which did not yet form a coherent whole. Babies learn with astonishing speed how to know a person, but they have parents watching over, drawing attention to important features, correcting them when they mistake a person for a toy or a tool.

By the time we are adults we are well advanced in the art of getting to know a person, but how do we get to know God? How do we extrapolate from our experience of 'knowing' a human person to get to know the one and only God who is invisible, inaudible and infinite? A Christian reply is that God speaks. Words, phrases, sentences lead us to a view of who God is, what his character is like, how he acts in situations. God speaks, and the scriptures are the primary, permanent source of his self-disclosure. But the Bible is too lengthy and detailed to be held in the mind as a ready frame of reference by which to check the data of our spiritual experience. The task of doctrine has been to summarise and highlight key points of revelation in a memorable form that becomes the skeleton of our knowledge about God.

Prayers structured round doctrinal themes

The written tradition of prayers in the Bible and in Christian liturgy and devotion demonstrates this most forcefully. Great prayers are built around doctrinal statements. Some evoke pictures of who God is: mighty creator, tender Father, jealous lover, victorious warrior. Others describe what he has done in the progressive themes of the biblical story: creating, redeeming, making covenants, sending his Son to die, raising him to life and pouring out the Spirit.

I used to dislike the phrase in doctrinal textbooks, 'the person and work of Christ'. It seemed a pompous and unnecessary distinction. Recently, however, I have been struck by the value of the double emphasis. There are the nouns which attempt to describe the eternal unchanging nature of the Son of God, and there are the verbs which refer to the story of his rescue mission in human history. They correlate with one another and often overlap. Jesus is the Great Shepherd of the sheep: the dynamic aspect of this is that he cares for us and gave his life for us. Often the 'being' words connect with the inner personal experiences in prayer. I-myself am gazing in wonder at the eternal mystery of the unchanging triune God who invites me to experience his presence and know and be known. The 'doing' words reconnect me to that numberless company which is the people of God in space and time. What God has done in the past in human affairs gives rise to the hope that he will do something congruent for us in days to come.

The Lord's Prayer illustrates this doctrinal structure

well. We begin by dwelling on our Father and his locus in heaven. We acclaim his holiness. We align ourselves with the repeated biblical themes of a God who comes to reign, whose will is to be done. Then, focusing on the twin doctrines of creation and redemption, we apply them in the present by praying for God to sustain us with food, to forgive our sin, and rescue us from evil's power.

Constant repetition of the Lord's Prayer, reading other biblical songs and prayers, hearing the carefully crafted collects which have been used in Christian worship down the centuries, such activities set these patterns of doctrinal themes in our minds. They provide a basis for recognising and relating to God in the same way that the skills for relating to people are learned in the nursery. Even in non-liturgical churches godly leaders tend to pray aloud in semi-liturgical patterns of prayer which are imbibed by the listeners. It does not take many months for a fresh, new church-attender to have a fairly settled idea in her head about what the content of prayer should be.

Prayer as a structured monologue

Many teachers and spiritual guides will suggest to a beginner that he set aside a regular daily time for prayer as a quiet inner monologue with a checklist of categories drawn from the examples of biblical prayers and traditional structures of worship. One such progression might be:

Praise	Starting by focusing on aspects of God's character. Acknowledging God's activities.
Thanksgiving	Matching God's character and activity to specific experiences and saying thank you for perceived blessings.
Confession	Admitting sinfulness, failure and specific sinful acts. Accepting God's forgiveness.
Petition	Asking God for grace and gifts which will lead to change in our character and circumstances.

| Intercession | Making similar requests on behalf of others. |
| Doxology | Some concluding phrases glorifying God and expressing faith in him (e.g., Amen). |

Prayer like this could be free-standing, but it is usually prefaced by reading a paragraph from the Bible and chewing it over robustly in the mind. Believers are encouraged first of all to address to the text questions which connect with doctrinal categories. What does this say about God and about his will for humanity and for the church? Then they are to move on to questions of application. How can these doctrines be applied to living in the modern world? Are there any ethical imperatives or promises of personal encouragement? The themes which have come into the mind during a time focused on a Bible passage become the content of the prayer which follows. Any length between ten minutes or sixty may be a recommended daily diet. Many Christians aim for half an hour, and occasionally achieve it.

Difficulties with a word-orientated spirituality

At this point I sense a chorus of protest welling up among my readers. There are many, many difficulties with this familiar approach to spirituality, questions that are begged and other well-worn traditions that are ignored. In what follows I would like to explore two of those difficulties.

God is different from us: his voice is not audible
Time and again in seminars on prayer, where I have developed the theme of knowing God and compared prayer with human conversation, someone has said, 'But my problem with prayer is precisely this: prayer is not like a conversation. God does not speak. There is nobody there. It is all happening in my mind. How do I know what is the voice of God?' Harry Williams expresses the problem with a stark illustration:

The medium of that transmission [of God's reality]

is something not unlike a ventriloquist's dummy. For
when God appears to speak to us in prayer it is we
who are putting words into his mouth . . . The cross of
prayer consists of accepting the humiliating fact that it
is by means of something like the ventriloquist's dummy
that God does in reality often get through to us, and in
recognizing that in any particular instance God may not
be getting through to us at all and we are left speaking
only to ourselves via the dummy.[2]

Down the centuries Christians have wrestled with the
tension Williams is highlighting, and have varied as to
how they are prepared to describe this area of faith and
experience. There are those today who prefer to reserve
the terminology 'God speaks' for words which come from
the scriptures. Only what was said through the prophets
and apostolic writers of the Christian canon is allowed
to be described as the words of God. The Holy Spirit
acts as a silent coach, nodding and prodding, highlighting
words from the Bible hidden in our hearts, encouraging
us inwardly to move in the direction God wants us to
go. True, there is often an inner dialogue when we are
at prayer, but both voices are our voices. 'Why are you
downcast, O my soul?' asked the psalmist. 'Why so dis-
turbed within me? Put your hope in God . . . ' (Ps. 42:5).
God's responses to our prayers, according to this school
of thought, are not words but gifts, new insight, more
love, accelerated healing, changed environments, maybe
even parking places. (The latter has become a touchstone
in a debate about the extent of divine intervention in
human affairs. Does God ever provide parking places for
harassed motorists who pray for them? A leading figure in
the Riding Lights Christian theatre company loves to tell
how he and a friend, late for an engagement, decided to
pray for a bus to come. Unfortunately they closed their
eyes and the bus shot past.)
Does God speak today? Some are saying no, but many
others reply yes. In this view there is no major discontinu-
ity between the experience of men and women in the Bible

and our experience today. When Jeremiah says that the word of the Lord came to him, when he 'saw' an almond branch and had a conversation with God about it (Jer. 1:4,11), he is not describing anything different from some of the more vivid moments which all of us have from time to time as part of a life of prayer. Jeremiah was a prophet; with the words and pictures came the conviction that they were not just for himself, but that he had God's authority to share them with a wider audience. He is a canonical prophet because, by the activity of the Holy Spirit, his book has been declared to be part of the authoritative word of God for every generation. But John 10 tells us that the sheep hear and recognise the voice of the Good Shepherd. Surely that means more (though not less) than a warm, obedient responsiveness to the text of the scripture. God still speaks today in individual hearts and still gives prophetic words to some for the benefit of others. We recognise his voice by faith and by its consistency with his revelation.

The best exponents of these positions are not far apart from one another, but the gap refuses to close. One side is concerned to guard against deceitful error creeping into the church under the guise of words from God through plausible and attention-seeking speakers. The other fears that such caution lacks the bravery and humility to admit that God does speak to us in a wide variety of ways, sometimes using the strangest people to be his messengers, and that he has not left us a fool-proof formula for distinguishing his voice from our own ventriloquist's trick. Both would want to reassure my anxious questioner that God is actively communicating and revealing himself in this generation in a way that is consistent with the biblical revelation. We have to walk steadily and trustfully by the Shepherd's side, getting used to the sound of his voice. Then we will shiver when we hear a stranger.

God is other than us and words cannot describe him

My first difficulty centred round God's words: if and how he speaks to us today. But another long-debated issue in spirituality is the adequacy of our words. Are words and therefore doctrines any help whatsoever in the quest for God? Is it possible to draw close to God by a word-based knowledge?

The mystical theology of the Eastern church has tended to put a great emphasis on what is called 'apophatic theology', a form of theology in which the emphasis is on what God is not. Positive doctrines have their use. With their images from our earthly experience, parent, ruler, lover, judge, they lead towards some knowledge of God, but it is very imperfect. There comes a point when in order to know God we have to proceed by 'unknowing', by recognising what God is not. He is not finite, not mortal, not comprehensible to the human intellect. There are possibilities of encounter with the living God which are best described by comparison with the experience of a baby, wrapped in the security of a loving embrace or gazing joyfully and intently into his mother's eyes. Adult intimacy can also have this quality.

Relationships, as I said before, may start with plenty of verbal exchanges, but for depth they require sight and touch and the silence of loving togetherness. The most popular books about prayer at the present moment are those which take seriously the longing of many people to be able to spend time alone, lovingly and lingeringly in the presence of God. They address the very practical problem that we find it difficult to do. Authors are searching through the long tradition of contemplative prayer in the church and attempting to distil its wisdom. A satisfying life of prayer tends to go, for instance, with a generally well-balanced state of health. Over-exhaustion or lack of exercise, slovenly posture or bad diet all militate against prayer in any depth. Then beyond these physical factors lie the questions of our moral and emotional state of health.

Guided retreats in the modern version of the Ignatian tradition are becoming part of a regular pattern for people in churches that might previously have been scornful about whether so much silence is a good use of precious time. A highly significant feature of such retreats is the combination of a doctrinal framework and freedom for the retreatants to start wherever they are. The director of an eight-day retreat will have in mind a progression of key gospel themes: the darkness of sin and the brightness of the loving grace of God; the call of Christ and our response as disciples; the suffering and death of Christ; the resurrection. Selected biblical passages that are likely to raise these themes are given to the retreatant daily. Warm comfortable beds, good food, a quiet house and a beautiful garden are usually provided.

Once the supports and pressures of normal life like work, family and friends are removed, the individual is starkly confronted with much of the internal noise of fear, anger, grief, desire and shame which constantly gets in the way of the love, joy, peace and trustfulness we think we ought to feel in response to a God who gave his own Son to die for us. Most of us run away from this conflict within ourselves most of the time. Hence the struggle we have with lack of concentration in prayer. The moment the pain level rises, we allow ourselves to be distracted. In the safe prayerful enclosure of a retreat, people find courage to confront their inner voices and the result is often an exhilarating and refreshing experience of prayer. It could, however, be dangerously overwhelming. At any point in time God knows the painful depths and deceitful corners of our human hearts, but we are not ready to be exposed to too much self-knowledge all at once. The Old Testament saints knew that if they were to be suddenly confronted with God in all his glory they would die.

Spirituality and psychology

The Reformers knew as well as the Counter-reformation figures like Ignatius that getting to know God is inextricably bound up with getting to know ourselves. Calvin acknowledges in the opening section of his *Institutes* that they are so closely connected it is difficult to say which comes first. But, as we have seen, knowing involves a world-view; so in every generation spirituality will be affected by the psychology of the prevailing culture.

We have had more than a century of a scientific exploration of psychology. Clinical data has been painstakingly collected. While much of it confirms what the poets and pastors always suspected, some of it has highlighted things they were inclined to overlook. Even the last few decades have seen amazing advances in our physiological understanding of the brain. The experiments indicated a division of function between the left side of the brain, with its control of more conceptual, linear and logical activities, and the right side of the brain, which deals with more emotive aspects of images, symbols, stories and lateral connections. It has become more natural for us to think in those categories than for previous generations, and we are more aware that certain types of education can emphasise one function to the detriment of the other. We need to give full attention to both if we are to do justice to the gifts of the creator. It is easy for spurious value judgements in favour of our preferred mode to creep in unnoticed. Theologians who write the doctrinal textbooks tend to be highly biased in the left-brain direction, though this is shifting as the issue has come into the limelight and people are experimenting with new styles of writing or 'doing' theology. Times of change are also times of insecurity. How do we ensure we do not lose essential guy ropes for the faith? At least it has been encouraging to see how well the material in the Bible itself covers the range of preferences, from Paul's lengthy and highly condensed sentences to the repeated apocalyptic visions in the book of Revelation. Material in the life and teaching of Jesus comes satisfyingly in the middle.

Christian pastors and spiritual guides have also learned a great deal from watching the struggles of psychotherapists as they try to disentangle how problems of the personality can best be overcome. Recently the pastoral theologian Thomas Oden has taken great delight in revealing how many of Jung's insights are to be found in the *Pastoral Rule* of Gregory, a leading textbook in the church for a thousand years. Oden is not belittling the wisdom of Jung. He takes a good look at the psychotherapeutic method of counselling and suggests it rests on something which has no basis without the doctrinal stance of a Christian to undergird it.

The therapist places herself imaginatively in the client's frame of reference and shares his world of inner conflict, without being drawn into the distress. The client feels accepted not on the grounds that he is behaving well, but because every human person is valued. He finds it safe to feel things that were previously too alarming to own, and he begins to grow in self-acceptance and understanding. Christian doctrine tells us that God loves us. He enters our world, takes part in our suffering, shares the limits of human life and goes through death, but without being destroyed. His grace towards us encourages us to open up, confess our darkness and be changed.[3]

I draw attention to the comparison because a major issue in spirituality is how this change occurs. What is the connection between understanding doctrinal truths about God, having appropriate responses of trust and joyful love, and choosing to align our behaviour to his will? The various schools of psychotherapy have gone round and round this triangle of thought and feeling and behaviour, looking for the best starting-point, and have increasingly concluded that there is no simple progression. We are a complex unity, and different problems yield to different approaches.

Theologians, by the nature of their profession, are inclined to assume the priority of thought. Thus Calvin: 'We assign priority to doctrine, in which our religion is contained, since by it our salvation begins; but it must be transfused into our hearts, and pass into our conduct, and thus transform us . . . '[4] English theologians with a particularly strong cultural distaste for examining or displaying feelings are inclined to rearrange the triangle as thought followed by decision and action, with feelings trailing well behind. J. I. Packer expounds the psychology of John Owen, the sixteenth-century Oxford academic puritan, as 'man created for rational action and equipped with a trinity of faculties'. These are: first, understanding; second, will; and third, affection. Packer does, however, admit that 'no choice is ever made without some degree of affection'.[5]

The fact is that there are people in churches who are very well versed in, for instance, the doctrine that we are justified by grace through faith in Christ. They can discuss its finer points in house groups and get a great glow of satisfaction in knowing that others recognise they have a sound view of it. But it has not yet effected the tiniest iota of change in the anxious, legalistic perfectionism that dominates their lives. Each time they pray 'Our Father . . . ' their feelings remind them that God is an endlessly demanding unfair parent whose standards they must strive towards but which they always fail to meet. The breakthrough may come during an illustration in next week's sermon, but it is far more likely that it will be a concrete experience of grace in a human relationship that will begin to produce the change, and a doctrinal understanding of what is going on may come much later.

Christians today should not be surprised by the emerging interest in spirituality. God made us for himself, as Augustine said, and human hearts are restlessly groping after him. We need not be unduly alarmed that some of the things which have helped us in prayer or in character growth have close counterparts outside the church. But we should not weaken in our conviction that the God we thirst for is not a power we can control by action or by prayer. The God we seek sent his Son in human history to die for us and for our sin. He makes demands and gives us grace to respond to him in penitence and faith. He spoke in the past and he speaks today in his word and by his Spirit in our hearts and lives.

Christian doctrine is the bone structure of Christian spirituality. Without good bones we are flabby, feeble and prone to painful disaster. We make them strong by feeding on a good diet from the word of God and exercising them in a life of loving relationships, purposeful service and a

growing capacity for prayer as we glorify God and enjoy
him for ever.

Questions for discussion

1. At the centre of Christian belief is the cross and
   resurrection of Jesus Christ. What difference might
   there be between a spirituality which sees these doctrines as vital and one which mainly focuses on God
   as creator?
2. Jesus taught his followers to call God 'Abba' (Father).
   One of the tasks of a human parent is to help their children become progressively more independent. Does
   Christian maturity mean we grow spiritually more
   independent?
3. Try to think of some more examples of situations
   (real or imaginary) where somebody's behaviour is
   not consistent with their doctrine. What do you think
   would be most effective in bringing change in those
   situations? What roles do thought, feeling and action
   play in your suggestions?
4. What are some of the main reasons for doubt in the
   Christian life? How might you help someone who was
   experiencing deep doubts to pray?

For further reading

P. Adam, *Living the Trinity*, Grove Spirituality Series,
no. 1 (Nottingham: Grove Books, 1982)

A. E. McGrath, *Roots That Refresh: A Celebration of Reformation Spirituality* (London: Hodder & Stoughton,
1992)

Sr Margaret Magdalen, *Jesus – Man of Prayer* (London:
Hodder & Stoughton, 1987)

A. Netherwood, *The Voice of this Calling: An Evangelical*

Encounters the Spiritual Exercises of St Ignatius of Loyola (London: SPCK, 1990)

The Revd Vera Sinton is director of pastoral ministry in Wycliffe Hall, Oxford. She previously worked for the Universities and Colleges Christian Fellowship, and taught at All Nations Christian College. She is a contributor to *Jesus 2000* (Lion Publishing) and *Restoring the Vision*, ed. M. Tinker (Monarch). She has written for Scripture Union *Daily Notes* and *Third Way* magazine.

7

Doctrine and Ethics

David Atkinson

What is 'Ethics'?

'Ethics' describes the discipline of thinking systematically about morality. This involves moral reflection about what is going on in a particular situation, and moral deliberation concerning what action should be taken. The task of ethics is in part to analyse issues of right and wrong, good and bad, in human attitudes, motives, intentions, and actions, and in part to give an account of moral character. This double task assumes a certain standard of goodness and rightness, and certain moral norms by which conduct and character can be judged. This assumption depends in turn on certain more fundamental beliefs about the nature of human beings and about the nature of the world in which we live.

For Christian people, 'Christian ethics' describes the discipline of thinking systematically about Christian morality, that is about Christian conduct and Christian character. Much of Christian ethics, particularly in the Protestant traditions, has tended to concentrate on conduct, and has been developed in a problem-based way, seeking to apply principles and rules to situations of moral uncertainty. But this is by no means the whole story. In the Anglican tradition of the seventeenth-century Caroline divines, for example in the work of Jeremy Taylor in *The Great Examplar* and in *Rules and Exercises of Holy Living and Holy Dying*, the focus is on moral formation, and the development of character: on what we should *be* rather than on what we should *do*. In the past decade or so, Protestant ethics has also seen a recovery of what has come to be called 'character ethics', which has challenged the dominance of an ethics of principles and rules. One of the most prominent contemporary exponents is Stanley Hauerwas, whose prolific writings include *Vision and Virtue, Character and the Christian Life* and *A Community of Character*.[1] Some writers from a feminist perspective, Carol Gilligan,[2] to name one, and Grace Jantzen,[3] to name another, are also moving the focus away from rules, and rules-based concepts of justice, and towards a model of ethics based on personal relationship, connectedness and caring.

Both aspects of the task of Christian ethics, the being and the doing, depend on fundamental Christian beliefs about human beings and the nature of the world. As we shall seek to show in this essay, these fundamental beliefs, expressed in Christian doctrines, shape the ways Christians engage in moral reflection and moral deliberation, and think about Christian character and conduct.

The ways in which doctrines shape ethics can be illustrated in the following not uncommon pastoral situation.[4]

Jan, Ted and Brian

Jan and Ted were at college together, both from upper middle-class Christian families – hers evangelical, his Anglo-Catholic. Their relationship developed into an intimate and exclusive one, and they soon started living together. Jan felt guilty about her sexual relationship, wanting it, but not enjoying it much.

Plans were made for a big church wedding, though Jan was beginning to have second thoughts. However, things had gone too far; she was swept into marriage on the tide of other people's expectations.

Ted had a reasonable job. They settled down. Three children were born in the first five years. Jan was tied to the home, had little real joy in caring for the children, harboured a resentment against Ted for making her pregnant, experienced renewed guilt feelings about her earlier premarital sexual behaviour, and longed that life offered her something more.

Then Ted was made redundant, and the family had a very difficult few months of adjustment before part-time work became available on a greatly reduced salary. When the third child started school, Jan immediately got herself a job as a receptionist. She found she enjoyed this new independence. Her salary gave her a power over Ted. She also found that she was attractive to men – a new discovery for her. She had increasing numbers of working lunches with them – with one in particular; soon an affair began.

Jan's relationship with Ted got gradually worse. Eventually, in a blazing row, the truth about the affair came out and Ted walked out. After a few weeks apart, Ted tried to effect a reconciliation. They both tried. They went to a counsellor and tried. But they were driving each other to emotional exhaustion, and it was with enormous relief that they eventually decided to seek divorce. They had been married nine years. The actual divorce, however, was extremely painful for all the family, and left Jan, who retained custody of the children, with a deep sense of confusion, depression and guilt. This was compounded by the news about a year later that Ted had married again. Jan was lonely and angry. She linked up with a group of women from the church and began to come in touch again with some of the religious convictions of her youth. To cut a long story short, she came back to God. Faith began to mean much more again. In the context of a community of others who understood her, she began to discover something of emotional healing. She came to a clearer acknowledgement of her own responsibilities in the break-up of her marriage to Ted. In some way she came to repentance.

A couple of years later she met Brian, whose first wife

had died three years before. He became a member of the church she now attended. They became friends, and eventually lovers. Jan's own children were now adolescents, and Brian hesitated before becoming a father to them. But eventually they decided to marry. This at last felt like the real thing. They want to marry in church, and seek advice from their pastor.

Discussion

In considering a situation like this, there are many levels to the pastoral task.

At one level, there are the *ecclesiastical* questions associated with church discipline in relation to divorce and the remarriage of divorced persons in church. These are themselves questions that arise when we attempt to hold together the church's witness concerning marriage and the church's witness concerning sin, repentance, grace, forgiveness and the journey of faith. Our doctrine of the church and of ministry, of law and gospel, will influence our approach to these questions.

Then there are the specific *pastoral* questions concerning the advisability of the marriage between Jan and Brian: is this what God is calling them to at this stage of their life journey? How could God's will for them be discerned? Are there remaining obligations to Ted for which Jan still bears some moral responsibility? Will this step be in the interests of the children? Have the personal factors in Jan's life which contributed to the breakdown with Ted been sufficiently resolved? Our doctrine of humanity, of sin, of maturity, and growth will be important here.

Third, behind these pastoral questions lie *moral* questions concerning sexual relationships, concerning the nature of marriage – and the nature of *this* marriage – before God, concerning the permissibility of divorce and the permissibility of remarriage. There are questions related to the significance of the gospel of grace and forgiveness, and that in Christ all our sins do not merely accumulate against us. Does Jan's spiritual state change the context of these questions in a material way? In the moral analysis of this case, is there more information we need before we can make up our minds? Is it clear what the facts are? What moral values are at stake in the decision? What possible options are open to the couple; to the pastor? What would be the likely outcome of such options? For Jan? For Brian? For Ted? For the children? For the pastor? For the wider Christian community? For the watching world? Our doctrines of marriage, sexuality, and family are all involved, and it is not long before we discover that we are also exploring the doctrines of covenant and community, and then of the communion of persons within the Holy Trinity, and what that implies for human relationships, their love, faithfulness and freedom.

Fourth, there is a further set of questions concerning the relationship of this case and these people to the ongoing *Christian tradition* of thought about such questions. What is the biblical teaching on marriage, on divorce, on remarriage, on guilt and forgiveness? Here there are exegetical questions concerning, for example, the meaning of the Greek word *porneia* in Matthew 19:9. There are the hermeneutical questions concerning the apparent divergence in teaching between the synoptic authors on divorce, and between them and St Paul. Is the New Testament clear? There are the questions of the way in which to interpret the New Testament moral teaching. Is Jesus offering us a law, an ideal, a compromise? There are the questions of the relationship between the New Testament context of these discussions and our own. There are questions concerning the ways in which others in the church throughout the centuries have understood and used these texts, and the weight we are to place on these traditions. Our doctrines of scripture and of the church are involved here.

Fifth, and behind much of this, are questions concerning *Christian character*. What sort of people should we be? What sort of choices should Jan and Brian make? How can the choices of a person's life be woven into a story which illustrates what it means to be a disciple of Christ? As we explore this, we find we are dealing with fundamental questions concerning our *basic metaphors* for God, and the ways in which our understanding of God and his ways moulds the way we frame our understanding of Christian character, and so of the moral questions and of appropriate pastoral and ecclesiastical responses. If we approach God mostly as creator and lawgiver, we may see the moral life mostly in terms of moral rules, of sin, of falling short of divine ideals. If we approach God mostly in terms of saviour and redeemer, our focus may be more on grace, forgiveness, the possibilities of a new start. If we approach God primarily through the metaphor of reconciler and comforter, we may want to speak about the moral life mostly in terms of what is appropriate at this stage of a person's spiritual journey. Clearly all these metaphors have their place in our doctrine of God. The moral and pastoral task is how, in the light of what we are coming to know of him, we can best, in this pastoral situation, give expression to Christian character, that is to express allegiance to Christ. What does love to God and loving justice towards our neighbour now require?

Starting-points

An example like that of Jan, Ted and Brian illustrates not only how 'Christian ethics' is just one part of a larger Christian pastoral task, but also how each part of that task is affected by fundamental Christian doctrinal beliefs.

Not all Christians have approached the task of Christian ethics in the same way, and of course there are many other approaches to ethics than Christian ones. In due course, we will try to broaden out our analysis of the shape and task of Christian ethics, and look at other areas of life (with a brief glance at political, environmental, sexual and medical ethics). Before we do so, however, we will pause to illustrate some of this variety of Christian and other starting-points for ethical enquiry.

In the pre-Christian world of ancient Greece, for example, ethics derived from rational reflection on what made for the best – that is, the most valuable and satisfying –

state of affairs for a human individual in his community. In the Old Testament, as we shall see in more detail below, ethics was intimately related to spirituality, and rested on the revelation of God's will to his people in the Torah. The people of God were to respond in obedience to the grace of God in his covenant and law. With the coming of Christ, Torah ethics were swallowed up in 'Spirit' ethics, and in the New Testament we find an understanding of morality, still part of spirituality, in terms of the new life of the Holy Spirit within believers who are united with the risen Christ in the community of his body, the church.

Within the course of Christian history there have been different ways of approaching ethical questions. In the Middle Ages, St Thomas Aquinas, whose work formed the basis for Catholic moral thinking, synthesised the 'natural' virtues as taught by Aristotle (prudence, fortitude, temperance and justice), with the 'theological' virtues of faith, hope and love. His approach to Christian ethics was by way of 'natural law', seeking to read what the will and purposes of God the creator – and therefore what moral imperatives for human life and community – might be, from an understanding of human nature and human needs. The Reformers, especially Luther and Calvin, began with a theology of the revelation of God's will in the scriptures, and understood the moral life in terms both of God's moral law and Christ's gospel.

Since the rise of deism, and the Enlightenment of the late seventeenth century, Western ethical systems have largely been based on secular philosophies. The many different starting-points have been not God and his will, whether expressed through natural law or special revelation, but the minds, emotions or wills of human beings, or human society, or the natural world. Some philosophers have sought to base moral theories on the power of human reason alone: moral obligation is discerned intuitively by the power of the mind (I. Kant). Others have begun with human emotion, arguing, for example, that pleasure is the highest good (Jeremy Bentham), or that there is a moral obligation to seek the greatest happiness of the greatest number (J. S. Mill). A third group begin with the power of the human will, believing that people must create their own morality by their own choices (J-P. Sartre), whether this is understood individualistically or whether we believe this could lead to a decision to prescribe morality for others.

Some ethics take 'nature', or the theory of evolution (A. Flew, J. Huxley) as the starting-point, arguing that 'what is good' must be defined in terms of 'acting in accordance with nature'. Some focus on the motives or actions of individuals, interpreting moral capacity in psychological terms (S. Freud). Others (K. Marx) begin with the community as the unit of goodness and are less concerned with individual choices, attitudes and behaviour.

Some secular moralities operate with a concept of moral objectivity. In other words, that there is an objective, 'outside', standard of moral obligation by which human beings can judge their moral choices. Others are entirely relativistic, believing that standards of right and wrong are matters of personal taste or private judgement and therefore that they vary from society to society and from person to person.

One major focus of moral philosophy in recent years has been an analysis of the meaning of moral language.

There are thus many different starting-points in ethics, and these reflect differences in fundamental beliefs. There are different beliefs about the source of moral obligation (God, nature, society, human beings); there are different beliefs about the nature of goodness (the character of God, the moral law, the direction of evolution, the happiness of the greatest number of people); there are different beliefs about the moral agent (are human beings the products only of their genes, their upbringing, their society, or are they responsible beings with freedom of choice, whose lives tell a moral story?); and there are different beliefs about the nature of the world (is this only a physical universe, a closed system of natural causes, or is there a supernatural dimension to good and evil, to judgement and grace, to divine and demonic power?).

Of this multiplicity of approaches to ethics, each reflects fundamental beliefs about the universe within which moral questions are raised, and about human nature – the character of the moral agent.

In the light of this we can now return to look in more detail at the question of what we mean by the term 'Christian ethics'.

What is 'Christian' ethics?

There is a distinctively Christian approach to ethics because there are distinctive Christian beliefs about the universe and about human nature and human society. In other words, our Christian doctrines of God, of creation, of sin and redemption, of the work of Christ and so on, give us a particular framework of beliefs within which moral questions are raised. Our doctrines of the will of God, of his character and purposes, for example, give us a particular understanding of the meaning of good and evil, right and wrong. Our doctrine of human nature, derived from our understanding of the image of God, of the incarnation of Christ and of our redemption in him, of our individual and corporate journey of faith through the power of the Holy Spirit from justification, through sanctification, to the kingdom of God's glory, gives a particular understanding of the moral life.

Sometimes, Christians come to the same moral conclusion about a particular situation as others who start from different fundamental beliefs. Many Christian moral values (e.g., the sanctity of human life, the value of truth-telling, respect for another's property or reputation, the importance of faithfulness in sexual relationships) may be shared by others who start with different basic beliefs. This need not be surprising if we believe that Christian values make for what is best for human flourishing in this world: others, from different starting beliefs, may come to similar conclusions about human well-being. What distinguishes Christian ethics, however, are the Christian beliefs with which we start, and the rationale on which it is based. Christian ethics is intimately linked to Christian doctrine.

Character

We need to be very careful, at this point, however. For the Christian faith is not just another philosophical system alongside others. Christian faith is Christian life. And there is no separate discipline called 'Christian ethics' which exists apart from the whole of the Christian life. There is no biblical book of ethics. The Bible is given to us as a way of understanding God, living for God, worshipping God. And Christian morality (and so the ethics which describes it) cannot be separated from the renewal of our minds by the truth of God, from the power of the Spirit within the church to help us live for God, from the goal of all our actions in the glory of God. Morality, doctrine, spirituality and worship are all aspects of one another. Christian ethics is not concerned with the detached application of principles to problems; it is concerned with the development of moral vision and character, with life lived in response to the call of the living God.

H. H. Rowley put this well in his description of 'the good life' as it is presented to us in the Old Testament:

> [It] is the life that is lived in harmony with God's will and that expresses itself in daily life in the reflection of the character of God translated into the terms of human experience, that draws its inspiration and its strength from communion with God in the fellowship of his people, and in private experience, and that knows how to worship and praise him both in public and in the solitude of the heart.[5]

In New Testament terms, we should say that 'Christian ethics must arise from the gospel of Jesus Christ'.[6]

Oliver O'Donovan argues that Christian ethics depends upon that central affirmation of the gospel, the resurrection of Jesus Christ from the dead. In the first place, the resurrection is God's reaffirmation of his creation, and of humanity made in God's image. The creation order embodies God's purposes. The world and human beings should conform to the way God has made the world. This leads to a rejection of all that disrupts God's order, and points to a fuller life beyond this order, but which does not negate it. So, in the second place, the resurrection looks forward to our participation in God's redeemed world order through the life of the Holy Spirit. The creation and the kingdom belong together: 'in the resurrection of Christ creation is restored and the kingdom of God dawns'.[7] The Christian's moral life, then, is a participation in the renewal of God's universe, a renewal which touches us at the points of our moral agency, our choosing, judging and deciding. Our Christian freedom means our sharing in the moral authority of Christ, no longer as slaves but as sons. The Holy Spirit, says O'Donovan, 'forms and brings to expression the *appropriate pattern of free response to objective reality*',[8] a response which St Paul designates as 'love'. 'Love is the overall shape of Christian ethics, the form of human participation in created order.'[9] Love is itself ordered and shaped by the insights of the moral law – that which describes both the created order, and the character of God the creator, as these come to us in ways which require moral response.

Mystery

It is at this point that the distinctive Christian approach to ethical method needs underlining. Many of the secular approaches to ethics conceive of the world as essentially knowable through our own powers of human reasoning, and the ethical task as spelling out the moral issues, making a reasoned moral evaluation, and coming to a decision. While this process may be part of the task, the Christian needs to say more. For the Christian view of God's world is that it is not essentially knowable to sinful people, but that at its heart there is mystery. We see now 'through a glass darkly'. As Craig Dykstra puts it: 'The moral world is a world of mystery rather than a world of problems.'[10]

The love of God beckons us forward into the mystery of his being, sufficient of which has been made known to us in Christ to guide our allegiance. The moral task is the process of being related to, not only guided by, God. Our lives tell the story of our relationship with God, a story we usually describe by the word 'character'. In contrast to 'problem' ethics, Dykstra speaks of Christian ethics as 'visional' ethics, and writes:

> Decisions, choices and particular actions are not the first consideration in visional ethics. The foreground is occupied by questions concerning what we see and what it is that enables human beings to see more realistically. For visional ethics, action follows vision; and vision depends on character – a person thinking, reasoning, believing, feeling, willing and acting as a whole.[11]

To repeat, Christian ethics is not the detached application of principles to problems. It is concerned with the dimensions of Christian vision and moral character, from which moral actions flow, which are part of learning to love God with all our heart and soul and mind and strength, and our neighbours as ourselves. That process of learning is not an individual journey. The doctrine of the church reminds us that it is 'with all the saints' (Eph. 3:18) that we come to know the love of Christ, and grow to maturity (Eph. 4:13), a process in which our 'faculties are trained by practice to distinguish good from evil' (Heb. 5:14, RSV). The church, in other words, is to be (in Hauerwas's phrase) a 'community of character'.

Doctrines and ethics

Within this framework, we can see how specific doctrines of the Old and New Testaments have relevance for the moral life.

For example, the doctrine of creation implies a certain divine order – both the physical order which the scientific enterprise seeks to understand and articulate, and the moral order which reflects God's character and the pattern of moral life appropriate for his creatures.

The doctrine of the fall warns us against claims to human autonomy and reminds us that there is an abnormality to the present world. We cannot simply read moral values off whatever just happens to be there.

The doctrines of the Trinity and of humanity in the image of God give a value to human persons and relationships, affirm human creativity, and tell us that we are stewards with responsibilities for the rest of the created world.

The Old Testament covenant within which God gives his moral law indicates that the moral life is to be understood in terms of obedient response to God's grace. The moral question is how best to express the covenanted steadfast love and faithfulness of God in our human contexts of moral choice.

The New Testament focus on the incarnation, life, teaching, death and resurrection of Jesus Christ, demonstrates the character of God within human life, and shows what faithful love means in action. It transposes the covenant ethics of the Old Testament into an ethic of new life in Christ.

The doctrine of grace is always linked to a call to live worthily in the light of the gospel of Christ, to shape every part of human living by the gospel of Christ. Within the struggle of human living and choosing within this fallen world, the Holy Spirit begins to renew our minds into the mind of Christ, direct our wills into line with the will of the Father, and strengthen us as we try to serve Christ within the family of the church.

The doctrine of the church reminds us of our interdependence in mutual ministry and mutual understanding, and also our mutual accountability. As a community of character, it is the context in which we learn habits of mind and behaviour which express our allegiance to Christ.

The expectation of the return of Christ is an affirmation that we are not trapped in a fatalistic determinism: our lives and choices matter, and our moral lives are set in a context of hope that God's created order will one day be fully re-established, and come to its completion under the Lordship of Christ as the kingdom of God's glory. That time is not yet here: we are still living under the constraints of a fallen world, this side of the Garden of Eden, and not yet in the new heaven and the new earth. Moral action will therefore have to take these constraints seriously. The actual will inevitably fall short of the ideal, and in the borderline situations of conflicting moral claims, our decisions may have to be those of lesser evils or greater goods, taken under the rubric of divine mercy and grace.

Christian conduct: principles and rules

It is only within the broader context of an ethic of vision, character, mystery and love, that it is appropriate to approach that other level of the ethical task, namely seeking moral principles to guide conduct. This part of the task of Christian ethics takes place in the conversation between Christian vision and 'faith seeking understanding', on the one hand, and the demands, adventures and difficulties of living in the modern world, on the other. We are now in a position to ask about the significance of Christian beliefs in framing specific moral principles and values. As we said earlier, the task of Christian ethics is not simply one of clarifying principles and then applying them in certain situations. Christian ethics is not to be understood in the legalistic way such an approach might suggest, but is rather the response of love to the gospel of Christ, the response of a life lived in allegiance to Jesus as Lord.

So where *do* moral principles, values and laws fit in?

The pattern of the Old Testament is instructive here. The primary statement about God is one of grace: 'I am the Lord your God, who brought you out of the land of Egypt, out of the land of slavery' (Exod. 20:2). It is within that context that the law is given: 'You shall have no other gods before me . . . ' (Exod. 20:3ff.). The law then describes the appropriate character and pattern of life for people whom God has redeemed. It reflects the character of God, and illustrates what an appropriate response will be in certain situations. The moral life is then expressed in terms of the story of the response of the people of God, how they learned more of him, fell away from him, were brought back into fellowship, and so on.

It is this law within the covenant relationship to which the prophets appealed in bringing their words of judgement and promise. This law is summarised by Jesus in terms of two Old Testament references to love: love to God (Deut. 6:5), and love to neighbour (Lev. 19:18). And the social expression of neighbour-love is justice (cf. Mic. 6:8). The moral law, then, tells us the shape of love in certain situations. And sinful human beings need that guidance to guard them against self-indulgence, or self-deception. But the moral life is not itself to be described primarily in terms of obedience to law, but in terms of loving allegiance to a person, and the quest for the sort of justice which expresses neighbour-love in all human affairs.

What shape would the response of love and justice have in certain specific moral settings? What would covenanted faithful love mean in these contexts? What does allegiance to Christ and the expression of love and justice to our neighbours require of us? That is the way the ethical question concerning Christian conduct is framed. We will explore in brief outline some of the moral principles and values which are relevant to four specific areas of moral decision: political ethics, environmental ethics, sexual ethics, medical ethics. We cannot here do any more than merely hint at the sort of doctrinal issues which such moral questions entail: our list is by no means exhaustive.

Political ethics
Moral issues raised under this heading include the concept of the state and the powers and limits of political authority (what is the state for in the purposes of God?). They include the enforcement of morality by civil law, including

questions of censorship. They include punishment, and the possibilities of resistance to state authority through civil disobedience, anarchy or terrorism; the legitimacy of war, and in what circumstances, also derives in part from the doctrine of the state. They include economic ethics, and questions of property, work, and leisure.

For a Christian, behind such questions lies not only a biblical doctrine of the state (which would draw on the relationship of Jesus to the Jewish state, his attitude before Pilate, St Paul's argument in Romans 13, as well as the picture of the demonic totalitarian state in the book of Revelation), but there are also more fundamental questions of order, justice, righteousness and peace. A Christian approach to such questions will need a theology of divine order, justice, righteousness and peace by which to evaluate the human counterparts.

A theology of justice also underlies the concept of the just war, a set of criteria by which to regulate both the decision to go to war, and the limitations in waging a war required by the demands of justice. Just war thinking can also be applied to the concept of a just revolution, and to a just economic sanctions policy which seeks to impose international order without resort to armed conflict.

A theology of justice is also basic to a Christian evaluation of the morality of nuclear deterrence, and to the moral decision concerning the use of weapons of indiscriminate mass destruction.

A doctrine of work will depend on an understanding of the creativity of God, and the sort of human actions which correspond to the action of God, in other words a doctrine of providence. It will also need a doctrine of the sabbath, of rest and of worship.

Environmental ethics
The Christian doctrine of creation is clearly basic to an ethical analysis of environmental issues, but so is a doctrine of the fall and of human sin. We need to think theologically about human agency, and stewardship, and about the responsibilities of human beings in relation to

the rest of creation, in particular in relation to decisions concerning the conflicts between present necessity and future safety.

A Christian approach to the natural sciences raises questions of epistemology, of truth, of moral commitment, and of the place of human beings as 'priests' of nature, bringing the silent order of the universe to articulation. The development of technology raises questions not only about what we can do, but also about how we think of ourselves in relation to our environment. The more we see ourselves as interveners in the system, as problem-solvers who by mere application of technical expertise can deal with life's difficulties, the more our estimation of what we can do, rather than what we should do, becomes the touchstone of what we will do. When technological pride rears its head, as it did at the Tower of Babel, the results are often the breakdown of community.

Sexual ethics
What is the significance of sexuality – the basic differentiation between human beings into male and female? A theology of sex would need to draw on the doctrine of the creation of male and female in the divine image, on the importance of the physical, the body, the significance of mutuality and complementarity in male-female relationships as these are explored in various biblical settings, on a theology of friendship and the meaning of love, on a theology of the erotic, as for example illustrated by the Song of Songs; it would need to explore the meaning of creativity and procreativity, and the significance of marriage, parenthood and family.

What makes a marriage? Christians have answered this question in different ways, some drawing on sacramental theology derived from the doctrine of the mystical union between Christ and his church, others starting from the theology of the covenant relationship between God and his people which is often expressed, especially in the Old Testament, in marriage analogies.

What breaks a marriage? Can a valid marriage union

once made ever be broken? Should a marriage be broken, and if so in what circumstances? Our answers to these questions will depend on our doctrine of marriage in the first place, and also on our understanding of reconciliation, forgiveness and grace.

Our theologies of sexuality, of friendship, and of marriage will also govern our approach to questions of sexual relationships outside marriage, and to the moral judgements to be made concerning sexual and other relationships between people of the same sex.

The doctrine of creation indicates that love and creativity belong together in the character of God, and by analogy therefore belong together within the male-female relationship of marriage. This is the basis for the view that the unitive and procreative aspects of sexual intercourse belong together, a view which has implications for the moral judgements we make about contraception, artificial insemination and surrogate motherhood.

Medical ethics

Medical ethics is concerned with moral issues which arise in medical practice, specifically such questions as abortion, embryo research, contraception, genetic engineering, euthanasia, care of the dying, transplantation, reproductive technology, experimentation, truth-telling in diagnosis, patient's consent, confidentiality, the meaning of health, the allocation of resources.

Let us take the example of abortion. There are two primary moral questions. The first concerns the status of the human foetus and whether or not it is to be regarded as a person with the rights of a person. The second concerns the resolution of conflict between the rights of the foetus and other moral values such as the life, health or wishes of the mother, the rights of the father, the conscience of the medical staff, the cost to society.

For Christians, an analysis of these moral values will involve drawing on fundamental beliefs about, for example, human nature and personhood (which takes us to the doctrines of, e.g., humanity and the Trinity), about the value of human life from conception (which takes us to doctrines of, e.g., creation and incarnation), about human rights (which requires an analysis of the nature of justice in the light of the character of God's justice), about parenthood, conscience, compassion, social priorities, law – for all of which Christian theology provides a particular perspective.

At the other end of life, the issues are no less problematic. The definition of death itself raises theological as well as medical questions, so does the point at which treatment of the living should give way to caring for the dying. In the debates concerning the termination of life by choice (whether the assisted suicide of voluntary euthanasia, or the passive decision to 'let nature takes its course') theological questions concerning death, suffering, compassion, autonomy of choice, the meaning of 'voluntary', all form part of a Christian moral analysis.

Underlying many medical ethical decisions are certain assumptions about the meaning of health, and about the doctor-patient relationship. A theology of *shalom*, the Hebrew word which sums up God's purpose for human well-being at all levels of life and relationship (it means peace-which-is-built-on-justice), is relevant to the former. A theology of covenant obligations, and therefore the meaning of faithfulness in professional relationships, will help to clarify the latter.

Conclusion

In a brief survey of this sort, we clearly cannot develop a careful moral analysis of each issue. What should be clear, however, is the intimate link between fundamental doctrinal beliefs, and the specific shape each moral question will take.

Whether at the 'meta-ethical' level of fundamental questions about the meaning of right and wrong, good and bad, or at the 'normative' level concerned with framing moral principles and moral rules, or indeed at the specific level of making a particular moral decision, our Christian doctrines determine our ethics. For Christian ethics is an aspect of Christian theology; an aspect, that is, of learning to love God with our minds. Christian ethics is that task of reflecting on and deliberating on Christian character and Christian conduct, in response to the love of God towards us in Christ. It is this which helps us fill out in any particular context how our love to God should show itself in love to neighbour and in the quest for justice, righteousness and *shalom* in human affairs.

Questions for discussion

1. Do you agree that the way we think of God affects the way we think of the moral life? Can you give some examples?
2. 'The way we are (character) is more important than what we do (conduct).' Do you agree?
3. Are there ways in which your church can help people grow Christian characters?
4. Are there any local moral issues on which your church could bring Christian beliefs to bear in a constructive way? What could you do?

For further reading

D. Atkinson, *Pastoral Ethics in Practice* (Eastbourne: Monarch, 1989)

P. Baelz, *Ethics and Belief* (London: Sheldon Press, 1977)

D. Brown, *Choices* (Oxford: Basil Blackwell, 1983)

D. Cook, *The Moral Maze* (London: SPCK, 1983)

C. Dykstra, *Vision and Character* (New York: Paulist Press, 1981)

R. Higginson, *Dilemmas* (London: Hodder & Stoughton, 1987)

O. M. T. O'Donovan, *Resurrection and Moral Order* (Leicester: Inter-Varsity Press, 1986)

Revd Dr David Atkinson. After postgraduate work in organic chemistry, he trained for the ordained ministry of the Church of England. Curacies in Bolton and Birmingham were followed by three years as Librarian of Latimer House, after which he was Fellow and Chaplain of Corpus Christi College, Oxford. He was visiting Lecturer at Wycliffe Hall, and helped to found the Oxford Christian Institute for Counselling. He has written on Ruth, Genesis 1–11, and Job for the Bible Speaks Today series (IVP), books on marriage and sexual ethics; war, justice and peace; and some aspects of medical ethics. He is co-editing a Dictionary of Christian Ethics and Pastoral Theology, and writing a book on the theology of counselling. He is now Canon Chancellor and Missioner of Southwark Cathedral.

8

Teaching Doctrine

Gordon Kuhrt

This final chapter seeks to draw together some of the important conclusions from earlier chapters, and their implications. We shall review the importance of doctrine both in the Bible and in the ministry of Christian leaders. We shall ask how doctrine is learned, and how it is to be preached and taught. '"What is truth?" said jesting Pilate, and did not stay for an answer.' So Francis Bacon put it. In our age 'truth' is often regarded as what each person happens to think. Not so for the Christian . . .

Truth and error: a biblical framework

Truth is of the utmost importance. The Christian faith arises from divine revelation and not from human speculation. This is what Paul meant when he said that the world by wisdom cannot know God. Of course there are things about God which the world shows us, as Paul says in Romans 1. We are part of God's creation, made in his image, with minds that can think. But these minds are darkened, and we receive the truth only as the Holy Spirit renews our minds (1 Cor. 1–2).

Thus the followers of Jesus 'were included in Christ' when they 'heard the word of truth', the good news of salvation (Eph. 1:13). Jesus is himself God's supreme revelation, his Word, the light of the world, full of truth. The Holy Spirit is called the Spirit of truth, but his work is not accepted or recognised by the world which is opposed to God.

Truth is therefore vital for Christian formation and growth. Jesus said that the way of discipleship was to follow his teaching. 'Then you will know the truth, and the truth will set you free' (John 8:32). God's gift of church leaders is so that the body of Christ may be built up towards unity in the faith and maturity in Christ. Then, 'speaking the truth in love, we will in all things grow up into him who is the Head, that is, Christ' (Eph. 4:15).

Jesus and the apostles demonstrated their concern for the truth by regularly arguing against false teaching. Jesus was by no means 'meek and mild' when it came to ideas that would mislead others about God and his salvation. In his book *Christ the Controversialist*, John Stott expounds the important arguments Jesus engaged in, particularly with the Pharisees and Sadducees.[1] So too Paul engaged in fierce controversy with false teaching in several of his letters (e.g., Galatians and Colossians).

The Bible gives some guidelines about responding to false teaching. First, the apostles repeatedly emphasised the importance of standing firm in the truth and holding fast to the gospel tradition. Timothy was urged to guard the truth. The early Christians were warned not to be led astray by strange teaching (e.g., 1 Cor. 15:2; 2 Thess. 2:15; 1 Tim. 6:20; 2 Tim 1:14; Heb. 13:9).

Second, the ministry and gift of teaching is very important. The truth is to be preached and taught faithfully, constantly. The gift of prophecy (building others up through the word of God) is of supreme significance, and church leaders should be 'able to teach'. The selection, training and encouragement of new generations of Christian teachers is of great importance – see 2 Timothy 2:2.

Third, just as Jesus himself and Paul the apostle engaged in controversy against false teaching, so church leaders are commanded to fulfil this duty and ministry. They are not only to encourage others with sound doctrine, but also to refute those who oppose it (Tit. 1:9). They must watch out for deceivers who do not continue in the teaching of Christ, and they must contend for the faith (2 John 7–11; Jude 3). Although the Christian faith encourages freedom of religion and worship, and surely leads us to deplore witch-hunts, inquisition and religious persecution, nevertheless, the church's teachers are called to teach God's truth, and to protect Christ's flock from wolves who will bring confusion and destruction.[2]

Teaching and doctrine: the Ordinal

In its official Formularies, the Church of England recognises this importance of teaching truth. When the Church of England ordains deacons, the Epistle reading is Romans 12:1–12, which includes 'Do not be conformed to this world but be transformed by the renewal of your *mind*, that you may prove what is the will of God, what is good and acceptable and perfect' (v. 2, RSV). Part of the deacon's work is to 'preach the word of God' and the 'doctrine of the Christian faith' and to be diligent in study so as to 'uphold the truth of the Gospel against error'.[3] This emphasis is repeated when priests (also called presbyters) are ordained. They are to 'proclaim the word of the Lord . . . teach and encourage by word and example . . . do all in your power to bring them [sc. the congregation] to loving obedience to Christ'.[4] Again, it is found in the Ordination or Consecration of Bishops. The Epistle reading from 2 Corinthians 4:1–10 speaks of not distorting 'the word of God' and 'only by declaring the truth openly do we recommend ourselves' (v. 2, NEB). The Bishop-elect declares (as do all clergy before ordination and appointment to office): 'I . . . declare my belief in the faith which is revealed in the holy Scriptures and set forth in the catholic creeds and to which the historic formularies of the Church of England bear witness'. The declaration speaks explicitly of a bishop's special responsibility to guard the church's faith. In the ordination prayer the

Archbishop prays: 'make him wise as a teacher, and steadfast as a guardian of its [sc. the church's] faith and sacraments'.[5]

The primary emphasis is on the *teaching* office of the bishop in a pastoral setting, and his duty to maintain the faith. This is the summary conclusion of the Archbishops' Group on the Episcopate 1990[6] when commenting on the 1662 liturgy of consecration. They cite the following evidence:

- the Collect asks for grace that the bishop 'may diligently preach the Word, and duly administer the godly discipline thereof'.
- three questions are addressed to the bishop-elect concerning the faith of the Church, the teaching office of the bishop and the exercise of discipline in relation to false doctrine.
- the prayer that precedes the laying on of hands asks in the first instance for grace that the bishop-elect 'may evermore be ready to spread abroad thy Gospel'.
- at the presentation of the Bible, the bishop is charged first to 'Give heed to reading, exhortation and doctrine'.
- the first function to which specific reference is made in the post-communion Collect is to 'preaching the Word'.

They then say that the Alternative Service Book (1980) 'makes no departure from the understanding of a bishop's office in the Book of Common Prayer'.[7]

Later, in their consideration of the theology of episcopal ministry the Archbishops' Group include a major section on 'the Ministry of the Word'. The ASB rite continues to require the bishop-elect to make a promise in answer to the Archbishop's question, 'Will you be diligent in prayer, in reading holy Scripture, and in all studies that will deepen your faith and fit you to uphold the truth of the Gospel against error?'[8] 'It is', they add, 'an important aspect of the feeding of his sheep that the bishop should seek to preserve from any anxiety which may seem to threaten their faith, those who have no means of assessing what sometimes may appear to be negative implications of what scholarship may seem to be saying about the fundamentals of Christian belief.'9

All this implies how very important Christian doctrine is.

The relevance of doctrine

The earlier chapters have argued cogently that doctrine is an essential part of Christianity. The vague dream of a Christianity without doctrine is but a mirage. Vera Sinton (p. 103) has mentioned the prayer attributed to Jesus Christ in John 17 with its famous words (v. 3), 'this is eternal life: that they may know you, the only true God, and Jesus Christ, whom you have sent'. Here we find claims about truth ('the only true God'), history ('Jesus Christ, whom you have sent'), and meaning ('this is eternal life').

The mind must not be neglected, but always kept associated with the emotions and the will. Relationships and discipleship are of the essence of Christianity, but so is the 'teaching of the faith'. Prayer and practical service are essential to healthy Christian development, but so is true doctrine.

The aim of this book is not to belittle or marginalise these other aspects of Christian faith and life. They are important, even vital, and so is doctrine. We are called to love God with our *minds* as well as heart, soul and strength. So we attempt to redress a balance – to demonstrate that doctrine is not only necessary but significant, relevant and essential to understanding the Bible, interpreting our experience, sharing and nurturing faith in evangelism, informing worship, structuring spirituality, and undergirding ethics.

How is doctrine learned?

Through worship
The Christian community gathers to worship God. This

activity makes use of words and actions, often occurs in a special setting, and is led by an ordained or chosen minister.

As we have seen in chapter 5, the form of the liturgy and the sacraments of baptism and Holy Communion are major purveyors of doctrine – for example, the holiness and love of God in confession and absolution, the necessity of new life through washing and the Holy Spirit in baptism, the centrality of the death of Christ in the eucharist. Many churches use the creeds of the early church which summarise Christian doctrine – particularly about the nature of Jesus Christ.

Hymns are an important, if frequently unconscious, source of Christian teaching. Both older traditional hymns and newer 'charismatic' songs vary considerably, of course, in their doctrinal content and value. (The sermon will be considered later in this chapter.)

However, quite apart from these words and actions in liturgy and sacrament, people learn about the Christian faith from the church building, its furnishings and layout, its ethos (music, light, etc.), its ministers and the way people relate to one another. Some 'older' Christians may take these matters for granted, but they need to ask very carefully: 'What does our church and its worship say about God, his relationship to us, about his people and their relationships to others? What impressions or ideas do they convey about Jesus Christ and about the Holy Spirit?'

The *way* in which the Bible is read, the prayers are led and the hymns are sung may more significantly shape doctrine than sermons about scripture, prayer and worship.

Through pastoral practice
It is often claimed that 'actions speak louder than words'. There are a whole range of doctrinal matters which can be systematically taught but which are much more likely to be learned by the *way* in which they are approached by the clergy and other church leaders. This would probably be seen in Christian initiation – baptism, confirmation and admission to Holy Communion – in attitudes to

healing ministry, sharing of church leadership, marriage and divorce, death and bereavement, and in the social and ecumenical dimensions of church life.

Pastoral practice will almost certainly speak louder than words in sermons. Hopefully the practice and the sermons will be consistent and inform each other, but if they are in conflict there can be little doubt which will have greater influence.

Through relationships
Much understanding of Christian faith is caught rather than taught. It is picked up almost unconsciously from parents, clergy, friends and Sunday school or youth leaders, or even from school teachers. What they say, how they say it – and, perhaps even more importantly, how they live – will contribute especially to youthful understanding (and misunderstanding).

The development of house-groups, discussion-groups, prayer-groups, etc., has been very significant in recent years. Many people appear to learn more in these less structured situations where conversation is the primary means of communication. To what extent this is tied in with scripture and 'orthodox' Christian teaching will vary very considerably.

Through personal reflection
Some people learn in very significant ways through private reading of scripture and other Christian literature, listening to tape-recorded sermons and talks, and by personal reflection, meditation and prayer. The personal presuppositions which are an important part of one's mental furniture will have been framed by personal response to the world as it has been experienced, its culture and its relationships. (Further attention to the relationship of presuppositions to Christian doctrine will be given below.)

Doctrine in preaching

We have seen how important doctrine and truthfulness are seen to be in the Bible, and the major role that the

Ordinal assigns to teaching the faith. We have seen again how important and relevant doctrine is to Christian faith and life. How, then, is it to be taught? In the previous section we noted the significance of worship, pastoral practice, relationships and personal reflection. Each is important and can be very valuable. But they have their weaknesses and inadequacies. Their roles are to complement preaching rather than to be substitutes for it.

In this section we will argue that preaching has been and should continue to be a major method of communicating Christian doctrine. However, even the very best preaching will only be one aspect of the learning process. It is vital for preachers and members of congregations to be aware of the complexity of the learning processes. It should be a salutary warning against complacency among preachers to discover how low down Christian people place preaching as a way of learning Christian doctrine.[10]

Preaching can certainly play a major role in teaching doctrine where the preacher and the congregation take the matter seriously. Just as doctrine will be conveyed (even unconsciously) through patterns of worship, the building and the ministry, so doctrine will be taught even through a sermon that has no such intention. It will be implicit in the treatment of the scriptures, even in stories and illustrations.

One of the major reasons for suspicion about doctrine in preaching is the perceived danger of the preacher *imposing* a doctrinal framework on the text. It is vital to recognise that we do all have an interpretative framework. 'Doctrine' is an interpretative framework. All of us, therefore, operate within a doctrinal perspective. It is not a matter of the preacher imposing doctrine on us, but of helping us to recognise the doctrine we already hold, and see if it is right.

The interpretative framework

All human beings think and respond by means of some kind of interpretative framework. Some of this may be almost instinctive. The more complex the matter about which we are thinking or to which we are responding, the more inevitably we shall respond by means of some interpretative grid, model, pattern or framework.

Take the example of meeting someone for the first time. How do we get to know them? We will use quite different approaches in the early moments – looks (either the face, posture, or bearing), voice and/or diction, personality or demeanour, clothing or some aspects of their apparent reactions to other people or to us. Different people use different frameworks depending on their interests, age, culture, and so on.

A similar range of approaches is possible when we hear someone speaking about national (or local) government. We may make a preliminary judgement on the basis of appearance or voice, or whether they represent a particular political party or grouping, or whether they mention, advocate or oppose a particular cause or stance which may be political, social, economic, industrial, or educational. In both cases we need to check our preliminary judgement by critical reflection.

So it is when we read or listen to any part of the Bible or a sermon or talk. We all inevitably come with our own very personal presuppositions – our views, ideas and prejudices. These will be affected by our own context and background – historical, racial, sexual, social, educational, economic and political, and they need to be recognised and evaluated. These factors may play their roles in at least the following four groups:

- the original speaker/writer and/or editor
- the translator(s)
- the contemporary preacher
- the reader or members of the congregation/audience.

Not only does each one of these have their own set of contexts, but any verse or passage in the Bible has its own multiple contexts.

1. The Bible as a whole – so the general view of scripture will be significant.

2. The part of the Bible (i.e., Old or New Testament) – people have quite different views of the two testaments.

3. The type or genre of literature (i.e., history, prophecy, poetry, wisdom, gospel, parable, allegory, epistle, apocalyptic). Readers or listeners will have varying understandings of the appropriate ways of interpreting the different genres. This would be so if they emanated from our own time, culture and language. But the issues become far more complex when the time is two or three thousand years ago, the culture middle-east Semitic or Graeco-Roman and the original languages Hebrew, Aramaic and Greek.

4. The author – if known. The authorship of many Old Testament books is unknown. The four gospels are actually anonymous – even if the evidence for the correctness of their traditional titles can be demonstrated. But Paul, as an author, provokes a wide variety of reactions in many people, even before they have carefully read his correspondence.

5. General patterns of interpretation will include degrees of reverence for the text and presuppositions about the relationship of literal, historical, mythical and symbolic writing. The role of 'official' interpretation by creed, confession, church, Christian leader, or scholar, will vary, as will the place accorded to reason, commonsense, science or contemporary culture.

There is another set of crucially important interpretative frameworks. This is the general theological position and/or churchmanship of the reader or preacher. It may be broadly or determinedly catholic, liberal-catholic, liberal, radical, evangelical, reformed, charismatic, or a mixture of several of these. This general stance may have a bearing on the Bible translation used and recommended – for example, catholics and the Jerusalem Bible, evangelicals and the New International Version or Good News Bible, liberals and the Revised Standard Version or the Revised English Bible (the revised edition of the New English Bible).

Modifying our frameworks

Maturity leads to critical reflection on and modification of interpretative frameworks and models. New or young Christians may interpret everything in the light of the idea(s) and person or group through which they came to faith – issues will often appear black and white. But growing maturity will involve: the capacity for self-criticism and evaluation of one's own 'group' or 'setting'; a willingness to listen to and learn from others; seeing more of the picture (of the Bible and the faith); looking at the wider context, with both antecedents preceding and implications following; analysis of the most significant features which are relevant in the present situation or in facing a particular issue. This analysis will distinguish the significant features in the original context(s) of action, speech and subsequent writing and/or editing, and the significant features in this situation here and now.

This may all sound too complicated, but we neglect the issue of presuppositions at our peril. They are inevitable, whether we recognise it or not, and whether we like it or not. Better to recognise it and reflect on it.

All Christians believe (though interpreting the idea in various ways) that the Bible is God's word for his people and is vitally important to knowing his gospel and his ways. The Church of England puts it like this: 'Holy Scripture containeth all things necessary to salvation: so that whatsoever is not read therein, nor may be proved thereby, is not to be required of any man, that it should be believed as an article of the Faith, or to be thought requisite or necessary to salvation.'[11]

Because the Bible is a library of books coming from many authors, different cultures and times, and addressing very different audiences, issues and situations, it is all the more inevitable that readers and listeners will adopt some kind of interpretative framework or model. That will be a doctrinal framework. This is not wrong or embarrassing. However, the Christian preacher and teacher will see that it is a matter of the greatest import that people are assisted towards the most helpful framework or model. This will enable them to 'know the truth' (John 8:32) and 'to grow up into him who is the Head, that is, Christ' (Eph. 4:15).

The single model

There are several ways in which people approach the understanding of Christian truth. I have called one approach 'the single model' or focus, another approach is 'the multiple model'. We shall look at each.

A single controlling doctrine which provides the main framework for thinking has been a feature of many theological movements. This singularity has a strength of simplicity and a sharpness of clarity. Such theological schools have their favourite parts of the Bible. The weakness of such a single model is that it may neglect a complementary truth or emphasis.

The *Protestant reformed* tradition focuses on the doctrine of justification by faith through God's grace. Its favourite parts of the Bible are Paul's letters to the Romans and Galatians. It is open to the danger of neglecting the necessity of obedience, holiness and practical Christian works. Hence Martin Luther's famous remark about the letter of James as 'a right strawy epistle'.

The *catholic* tradition focuses on the doctrine of the church, its ministry and sacraments. Their special part of the Bible is Matthew 16:18–19, where Jesus says to his disciple, 'You are Peter [*petros*] and on this rock [*petra*] I will build my church, and the gates of Hades will not overcome it. I will give you the keys of the kingdom of heaven . . . ' It is open to the danger of uncritically identifying a historical institution, the Roman Church (with its bishop or Pope), with the body of Christ, and of arrogating a jurisdiction which leads to an abuse of power and a corruption of teachings in the Bible (e.g., the doctrines relating to the Virgin Mary and the infallibility of the Pope).

The *liberal* social gospel tradition particularly emphasises the love of God and looks to the parable of the Good Samaritan. There is nothing here about atonement or justification, church and sacraments – it's all about being good neighbours.

Liberation theology looks to the exodus tradition as its framework. God's supreme concern is seen as the freedom of those enslaved in any way, and wherever there is work towards such liberation, it is understood as being the Spirit of God at work in our world.

The *evangelical* traditions have, at times, made a primary model or focus of either the Bible or conversion. The key passage for those who see the former as a vital framework is 2 Timothy 3:16–17, 'All Scripture is God-breathed and is useful for teaching, rebuking, correcting and training in righteousness, so that the man of God may be thoroughly equipped for every good work.' The classic passages about conversion are either that concerning Paul on the Damascus road, or the story of Nicodemus and Jesus in John 3 – especially Jesus saying, 'I tell you the truth, no-one can see the kingdom of God unless he is born again' (v. 3), and 'For God so loved the world that he gave his one and only Son, that whoever believes in him shall not perish but have eternal life' (v. 16).

The *charismatic* movement has a primary framework in an experience (sometimes called the baptism) of the Holy Spirit, and so pays special attention to descriptions of this experience in the Acts of the Apostles and the words of John the Baptist, 'I baptise you with water for repentance. But after me will come one who . . . will baptise you with the Holy Spirit and with fire' (Matt. 3:11).

The advantages of such single models or frameworks is that they are usually memorable, often powerful, and give a sense of identity and clear purpose to a church, a group or a movement. However, as a movement or individual within it matures, the factors noted on page 148 will come into play. As the wider picture comes more into focus and other doctrinal emphases are grappled with, so it is inevitable that the sharp simple edges of the original model become a little less distinct and straightforward. The boundaries of the identity will become somewhat blurred, and the movement or individual faces the choice of further dialogue and openness to self-critical evaluation or retreat into a ghetto of rigidity, repression and isolation. A classic example of the latter is seen in the Exclusive Brethren groups.

There are other single or simple models which are not limited to a church or movement. These may be very valuable in a certain context. Examples might be:

1. 'Christianity is Christ' (i.e., he is its centre and focus). The plan of salvation centres on him, and so does the scripture. The Christian life is described as being 'in Christ'. Christian maturity is growth in him and becoming more like him.

2. 'Religion is grace' (i.e., it is supremely about God's undeserved love and mercy, and not primarily about either God's law or human good works or merit). The incarnation and especially the death of Jesus Christ demonstrate the gracious love of God, who seeks and saves those who are lost.

3. 'A baptised life' (i.e., baptism 'provides a pattern and shape for the baptised life'[12]). This is the life of Christ, life in and through Christ, Christian life, a converted life. Just as the marriage ceremony is a decisive event but must then be worked out through married life, so baptism is a decisive event but must be worked out through a baptised life. Baptism is into forgiveness, into Christ, into his death and resurrection, into (or with) the Holy Spirit, into adoption, and into the body of Christ.[13] This model is particularly powerful, since it enshrines all the encouragement God offers and clarifies all the commitment the disciple should make. It is the sacrament of initiation and is therefore, not surprisingly, a framework for life.

4. 'A eucharistic life' (i.e., a life in which meeting at the Lord's table constitutes and continually reconstitutes the spiritual reality of life in Christ). We do this to remember, and the remembering renews the reality of Christ and his death. We do this to feed on Christ, and so are renewed in our union with him. We do this in the Christian community, and so are renewed in the body of Christ. We do this 'until he comes', and so are renewed in the glorious hope of his return and the final consummation of the kingdom.

5. 'Ministry is service.' The word 'ministry' has been hijacked in the general public's perception by the ordained ministry. This is seen in almost all churches as a position, status or order of authority, leadership, teaching and pastoral responsibility. It involves oversight of the Christian congregation, and normally presiding at the eucharist or Holy Communion. The role of lay members is often seen as helping, assisting or serving 'the minister'. But Jesus, the Good Shepherd (pastor), the Bishop (overseer), the High Priest for all time, once said, 'whoever wants to become great among you must be your *servant*, and whoever wants to be first must be *slave* of all. For even the Son of Man did not come to be served, but to *serve*, and to *give* his life as a ransom for many' (Mark 10:43–5). All Christians are called to ministry (i.e., service of Christ, his church and world). All Christians receive spiritual gifts (charismata) for ministry.

The multiple model
The single or simple model is often inadequate as a vehicle for Christian truth and a means to Christian maturity. The whole truth will often require a balancing of partial truths which may at first appear to be conflicting but which will eventually be seen as complementary.

The most obvious example of the multiple model is the doctrine of *the Trinity*. This may appear difficult and complex, but down through the centuries Christians have been in widespread agreement that some expression of the unity-and-threeness or three-in-oneness of God is the only way to do justice to the full revelation of God's nature. On the one hand there is no doubt that God is one, creator and Lord of all. However, the early Christians could find no way to be true to Jesus Christ, to his authority, his teaching and his resurrection, other than by worshipping him as Lord and Saviour. Though he prayed to God the Father and was submissive to his will, there was also a oneness between them. So too with the Spirit. Those early Christians recognised evidence of a separateness, a distinct personal identity of one who comes from the Father and the Son, and came decisively upon Jesus in his earthly life, and was promised by Jesus as his continuing presence upon his disciples. Yet he is also the Spirit of God, and the Spirit of Jesus, sharing fully in the divine nature. Thus we acknowledge a multiple model as a framework for our doctrine of God and our experience of God – he is one and also three-in-one.[14]

There have been times in church history when Christians have moved towards the simplicity of making a single model of God's *unity*. Jesus is therefore regarded as essentially a human being who was *not* divine, and the Spirit is a created person or force. Such teaching was rejected by the mainstream church since it failed to incorporate the full range of New Testament language. It was called 'heresy'. However, although the traditional orthodox doctrine of the Trinity is complex, it soon became deeply embedded in the liturgy (see chapter 5). Baptism is in the name of God – the Father, the Son and the Holy Spirit (Matt. 28:19). A famous prayer is 'the grace of the Lord Jesus Christ, and the love of God, and the fellowship of the Holy Spirit be with you all' (2 Cor. 13:14). The Apostles' Creed and the Nicene Creed are both trinitarian in shape – as are many hymns and songs, traditional and contemporary.

A second example of the multiple model is the doctrine of the *person of Jesus Christ*. Who was he? Who is he? The traditional and classic Christian doctrine is that he was and is both fully divine and fully human. So the Nicene Creed asserts:

> We believe in one Lord, Jesus Christ,
> the only Son of God,
> eternally begotten of the Father,
> God from God, Light from Light,
> true God from true God,
> begotten, not made,
> of one Being with the Father.
> Through him all things were made.

This leaves us in no doubt about his full divinity, but the Creed goes on:

> he came down from heaven;
> by the power of the Holy Spirit
> he became incarnate of the Virgin Mary, and was
>   made man.
> For our sake he was crucified under Pontius Pilate;
> he suffered death and was buried.

This equally leaves us in no doubt about his full humanity. The writer of the Fourth Gospel summarised it thus: 'The Word was God . . . The Word became flesh' (John 1:1, 14).

The early Christians believed that this was no mere matter of abstruse theology. They believed the gospel was at stake – the reality and possibility of salvation. If Jesus was not God, he could not save (because only God can be a Saviour, only God can bring us back into his presence, family and forgiveness). But if Jesus was not human, humanity could not be saved (because it was the obedience and sacrifice of the human Jesus which opened the way for rebellious humanity to come 'through the veil' (Heb. 10:20) into the holy presence of Almighty God).

As with the doctrine of the Trinity, there have been times in the history of the church when Christians have settled for a single model of Christ's identity. They have emphasised his essential humanness and suggested that he was perhaps additionally endowed with the divine nature either at his baptism or at the resurrection. Others have so emphasised his divinity as to imply that his 'humanity' was only an 'appearance' but not a reality. Thus his suffering and death were essentially illusory. These attempts at simplicity and single models have been condemned as heretical. They do not fit the evidence. A multiple model is required – that Jesus is fully divine and fully human.[15]

This sort of model is important. Important because of truth, and important because of its implications for Christian life and growth. However, it needs careful teaching. We have seen how the Trinity is embedded in liturgy, hymnody and the creeds, and how the dual natures in Christ are emphatically demonstrated in the Nicene Creed. There are many Christian doctrines that require this kind of multiple model. Failure both to recognise this and to teach it leads to many brands of lopsided Christianity, unbalanced, and unhelpful, which prevent growth to maturity in both understanding and service. Christian teachers and people are called to have the kind of theological understanding that need not be vast in extent but ought to be *deep in integrity*. It must not mislead people in its assertions, its denials, or its balance. It is where complementary truths relate to one another that the Christian teacher must exercise special care and endeavour to find helpful and memorable models.

Here are some further examples.

1. *How is a person made right with God, or justified*? Is it by faith, or is it by works? We have seen earlier (p. 149) that the Reformation tradition often appeals to the model which stresses that we are justified by faith alone – the Latin phrase was *sola fide* (Rom. 5:1). But this simple answer has to be modified by saying that while faith is a gift of God's grace, so justification is by grace alone – *sola gratia* (Rom. 3:24). However, in his epistle James argues, 'What good is it . . . if a man claims to have faith but has no deeds? Can such faith save him? . . . You see that a person is justified by what he does and not by faith alone' (Jas. 2:14, 24). Paul says Abraham was justified by *faith* (Gal. 3:6–9), and James says he was justified by *works* (Jas. 2:21). It is simplistic to say they contradict each other. They are dealing with different issues, and their teaching can then be seen as complementary. The multiple model the preacher needs will be something like this: We become right with God *only* on the basis of God's *grace*, which can *only* be received by *faith*, which can *only* be genuine if good *works* follow.

2. *How should we regard the scriptures* – as the Word of God or the words of human beings? With reverence or with reason? Many Christians adopt a simple model that

it is God's word written, God-breathed (2 Tim. 3:16; cf. p. 150). This has sometimes been expressed in such a way as to imply that the human writers were almost unconscious, like a word-processor on to which the Holy Spirit 'dictated' the message. Since the eighteenth century, there has been a reaction to this. Instead, some say, the simple model is that the Bible is a library of human writings which portray in many and conflicting ways human experiences of and strivings for God. Readers, so the argument goes, must use their reason to sort out the wheat from the chaff.

A more complex multiple model will be to say that it is the word of God in and through the words of human beings.[16] Such a model can then do justice to the wide variety of genres in the Bible, the evidence of research (Luke 1:1–4), and of different literary styles and theological emphases, while at the same time recognising the coherence of God's saving covenant purpose, his revelation, his providence, and the gracious work of the Holy Spirit in the prophets and apostles.[17] This model recognises our Lord's endorsement of the prophetic Old Testament and preparation for the apostolic New Testament. So, reverence and reasonableness can walk together – though not always comfortably, but that need not surprise us. Whenever the infinite meets with the finite, there will be boundary problems. The nature of scripture has some parallels to the nature of the Lord Jesus himself. The point here, once again, is that a single model will not do.

3. *When is the kingdom of God*? Has the kingdom *now already* come, so that Christians live in its reality in the present; or is the kingdom *not yet* come, so that we look forward to its reality in the future?[18] Two famous scholars did adopt single models to answer this question. Albert Schweitzer argued that Jesus' teaching placed the coming of God's kingdom entirely in the future.[19] C. H. Dodd, on the other hand, argued that the kingdom broke into the world in the coming of Jesus because he preached, 'The time is fulfilled, the kingdom of God has arrived' and 'The kingdom of God has come upon you'

(Mark 1:15 Dodd's translation, and Matthew 12:28, with both verbs in the perfect tense).[20]

But these single models simply will not do. They involve distorting the evidence, which speaks of the kingdom both as a present reality and as a future expectation. Certainly it has come, for it 'is among you' or 'within you' (Luke 17:21) and is to be received like a child (Mark 10:15). Yet it is to be awaited, for Jesus taught the disciples to pray 'your kingdom come' (Matt. 6:10). In the parable of sheep and goats he speaks of the Son of Man coming in glory for judgement and saying to those who have ministered to the needy, 'take your inheritance, the kingdom prepared for you' (Matt. 25:34).

So, yet again, a multiple model is required – the kingdom is both now and yet to come. It has been inaugurated by Jesus but is to be consummated on his return. It has come, but not fully come. In Paul's letters, a similar double dimension is found concerning salvation, redemption and adoption. We have been saved, redeemed and become God's children, and yet we shall be saved by the life of Jesus, and 'we groan inwardly as we wait eagerly for our adoption . . . the redemption of our bodies' (Rom. 8:23).[21]

Now, these multiple models are not theological pedantry. They have very practical implications for Christian discipleship. A great divide often exists between those Christians who emphasise the present reality of God's reign and think little of its future completion, and those who look to the future consummation and appear to think little of its present significance. Take, for example, the following areas:[22]

- *Knowledge of God* – Christians can have confidence in what has already been revealed, especially in Christ and scripture, but need to have humility about what is not yet revealed or what is not known with clarity.
- *Holiness* – Christians are already in Christ, and are indwelt by the Spirit, who is producing his fruit in a changing character which is marked especially by love,

but they are not yet fully transformed into the likeness of Christ and free from the love of sin.

- *Health* – Christians already see some miracles of healing, and experience remarkable degrees of peace in heart and mind, but our bodies and minds are not yet free from pain, disease, weakness and death.
- *Church life* – Christians together form the body of Christ, the people of God marked by holiness and catholicity (as the Apostles' Creed says), but they are not yet free from sinfulness, division and false teaching.
- *Community life* – already the Spirit of God is at work in the world, restraining evil and enabling good, and many Christian people exercise a very significant effect as salt and light, but we do not yet see the reign of God in justice, righteousness and peace.

These are just a handful of instances. However, there are many other areas of Christian teaching where a lack of balance is frequently demonstrated because of failure to adopt such a multiple model. Take the following additional examples: the sovereignty of God and human responsibility; God – transcendent and immanent; word and Spirit; word and sacrament; humanity – in the image of God, fallen, redeemed; the atonement – metaphors which are objective and subjective; evangelism – personal and social.

In conclusion

We have seen that Christian people need to know the faith, and Christian leaders are urged to teach the faith, and to commend it and defend it. Christians need confidence in the faith. Confidence does not mean either arrogance or pride. Genuine knowledge will only derive from God's gracious revelation of himself, which we receive through the Holy Spirit's work. That leaves no place for self-confidence but, on the other hand, we must not be content with ignorance and insecurity where our loving heavenly

Father wants us to enjoy knowledge and assurance. In that sense we need to be confident in our handling of the great truths which shape the Christian faith. What are we saying about the faith? What are people hearing about doctrine? How are we preaching? How are we all learning? Michael Ramsey, a recent Archbishop of Canterbury, put it very concisely – 'Study – not to be erudite, but simple.'[23]

The task of doctrine is humbly and clearly to summarise and highlight the significant areas of Christian teaching in a way that is memorable and provides models for our understanding. In a nutshell, doctrine matters!

Questions for discussion

1. How can the ministry of teaching be given greater significance by both clergy and lay people?
2. Is the teaching office of the Bishop adequately recognised and exercised?
3. Are there areas of your church's life which teach doctrine in conflict with the Bible or the preaching?
4. How have you modified your interpretative framework through further Bible study and reflection?
5. How are either single or multiple models of Christian doctrine helpful in your Christian thinking and living?

For further reading

B. Milne, *Know the Truth* (Leicester: Inter-Varsity Press, 1982)

I. H. Marshall, *Biblical Inspiration* (London: Hodder & Stoughton, 1982)

J. R. W. Stott, *The Cross of Christ* (Leicester: Inter-Varsity Press, 1986)

J. R. W. Stott, *The Contemporary Christian* (Leicester: Inter-Varsity Press, 1992)

J. R. W. Stott, *I Believe in Preaching* (London: Hodder & Stoughton, 1982)

D. L. Edwards and J. R. W. Stott, *Essentials* (London: Hodder & Stoughton, 1988)

J. D. Douglas (ed.), *The Illustrated Bible Dictionary* (Leicester: Inter-Varsity Press, 1980)

Sinclair B. Ferguson and David F. Wright (eds), *New Dictionary of Theology* (Leicester: Inter-Varsity Press, 1988)

Joel B. Green and Scot McKnight (eds), *Dictionary of Jesus and the Gospels* (Leicester: Inter-Varsity Press, 1992)

Gordon Kuhrt was in parish ministry for twenty-two years before becoming Archdeacon of Lewisham in 1989. He has taught New Testament Studies for many years to Readers candidates, and for the University of London Extra-Mural Department. He has written two books, including *Believing in Baptism*, and contributed to others. He is a member of the General Synod and its Board of Ministry, is an Inspector of Theological Colleges and Courses, and on the Council and staff of the College of Preachers.

Notes

1 Why Doctrine?: The Confession of a Disillusioned Liberal

1 John Hick (ed.), *The Myth of God Incarnate* (London: SCM Press, 1977); James Barr, *Fundamentalism* (London: SCM Press, 1977).

2 Some of these points are developed at greater length in my book *Understanding Doctrine: Its Purpose and Relevance for Today* (London: Hodder & Stoughton, 1991). For two more scholarly approaches to the same issue, see George Lindbeck, *The Nature of Doctrine* (London: SPCK, 1984); Alister E. McGrath, *The Genesis of Doctrine* (Oxford: Basil Blackwell, 1990).

3 *Institutes of the Christian Religion*, 1. 6. 2.

4 This approach is vigorously defended in John Hick and Paul F. Knitter (eds.), *The Myth of Christian Uniqueness* (London: SCM Press, 1987), which – interestingly – failed to attract anything even approaching the same interest as John Hick (ed.), *The Myth of God Incarnate* (London: SCM Press, 1977). For a vigorous scholarly refutation of the pluralism of this approach, see Gavin D'Costa (ed.), *Christian Uniqueness Reconsidered: The Myth of a Pluralistic Theology of Religions* (Maryknoll, NY: Orbis Books, 1990).

5 C. S. Lewis, *Mere Christianity* (London: Collins, 1956), pp. 132–3.

6 Charles Gore, *The Incarnation of the Son of God* (London: John Murray, 1922), p. 23.

7 Letter cited in F. A. Iremonger, *William Temple* (London: Oxford University Press, 1948), p. 490.

8 Oliver O'Donovan, *Resurrection and Moral Order: An Outline for Evangelical Ethics* (Leicester: Inter-Varsity Press, 1986).

9 Gore, *The Incarnation of the Son of God*, p. 22.

4 Doctrine and Evangelism

1 William Abraham, *The Logic of Evangelism* (London: Hodder & Stoughton, 1989), p. 1.

2 Michael Marshall, *The Gospel Connection* (London: Darton, Longman & Todd, 1991), p. 30.

3 *The Measure of Mission* (London: Church House Publishing, 1987), p. 38.

4 Alister McGrath, 'The Eucharist: Reassessing Zwingli', *Theology* 93 (January-February, 1990), p. 15.

5 ibid., p. 18, citing Alasdair MacIntyre, *After Virtue*, 2nd ed. (Notre Dame, IN: University of Notre Dame Press, 1984) p. 197.

6 Evangelical Alliance Commission on Evangelism, *On the Other Side* (London: Scripture Union, 1968), p. 67.

7 Abraham, *The Logic of Evangelism*, p. 17.

5 Doctrine and Worship

1 Rowan Williams, *Eucharistic Sacrifice – The Roots of a Metaphor*, Grove Liturgical Study no. 31 (Nottingham: Grove Books, 1982), pp. 21–3.

2 The meaning of these terms is explained earlier, on pp. 82–3.

3 The text of this Proclamation is to be found in the Parker Society volume of the Liturgies of Edward VI, pp. 1–2, or in my own *Background Documents*

to *Liturgical Revision 1547–1549*, Grove Liturgical
   Study 35 (Nottingham: Grove Books, 1983), p. 14.
4 *The Alternative Service Book 1980*, p. 10.
5 See *The Final Report* (London: Catholic Truth
   Society/SPCK, 1982), pp. 11–16.
6 John Robinson, *Honest to God* (London: SCM
   Press, 1963).
7 J. L. Houlden's 'Liturgy and her Companions: A
   Theological Appraisal', in R. C. D. Jasper (ed.),
   The Eucharist Today: Studies on Series 3 (London:
   SPCK, 1974), pp. 170, 172–4.
8 Colin Buchanan, 'The Liturgist in the Church',
   in Peter Eaton (ed.), *The Trial of Faith* (London:
   Churchman, 1988), pp. 143–61.

6 Doctrine and Spirituality

1 J. Tiller, *Puritan, Pietist, Pentecostalist* (Nottingham:
   Grove Books, 1982), p. 5.
2 H. A. Williams, *Tensions* (London: Fount Books,
   1989), p. 42.
3 T. C. Oden, *Care of Souls in the Classic Tradition*
   (Philadelphia: Fortress Press, 1984).
4 Quoted in A. E. McGrath, *Roots That Refresh: A
   Celebration of Reformation Spirituality* (London:
   Hodder & Stoughton, 1992), p. 41.
5 J. I. Packer, *Among God's Giants* (Eastbourne:
   Kingsway, 1991), p. 256.

7 Doctrine and Ethics

1 S. Hauerwas, *Vision and Virtue: Essays on Christian
   Ethical Reflection* (Notre Dame, IN: University
   of Notre Dame Press, 1974), *Character and the
   Christian Life* (San Antonio, TX: Trinity, 1975),
   A Community of Character (Notre Dame, IN:
   University of Notre Dame Press, 1987).
2 C. Gilligan, *In a Different Voice: Psychological*

Theory and Women's Development (Cambridge, MA; London: Harvard University Press, 1982).

3 G. Jantzen, 'Connection or Competition: Identity and Personhood in Christian Ethics' in *Studies in Christian Ethics* Vol. 5, No. 1 (Edinburgh: T. & T. Clark, 1992).

4 Freely adapted, with permission, from Lewis B. Smedes' course notes, 'Cases for Moral Decision Making', Fuller Seminary, 1989.

5 H. H. Rowley, *The Faith of Israel* (London: SCM Press, 1956), p. 149.

6 O. M. T. O'Donovan, *Resurrection and Moral Order* (Leicester: Inter-Varsity Press, 1986), p. 11.

7 ibid., p. 15.

8 ibid., p. 25.

9 ibid., p. 25.

10 Craig Dykstra, *Vision and Character* (New York: Paulist Press, 1981), p. 36.

11 ibid., p. 59.

8   Teaching Doctrine

1 John Stott, *Christ the Controversialist* (London: Inter-Varsity Press, 1970).

2 See further my chapter 'Principled Comprehensiveness' in A. F. Gibson (ed.), *The Church and its Unity* (Leicester: Inter-Varsity Press, 1992), pp. 132ff.

3 The Alternative Service Book 1980 (ASB), pp. 344–5.

4 ibid., pp. 356–7.

5 ibid., pp. 388, 394.

6 *Episcopal Ministry*, The Report of the Archbishop's Group on the Episcopate (London: Church House Publishing, 1990), pp. 81ff.

7 ibid., pp. 89ff.

8 ASB, p. 389.

9 *Episcopal Ministry*, p. 90.

10 This was painfully discovered through specific enquiry.

11 Article 6 of the Thirty-Nine Articles (found at the back of the Book of Common Prayer).

12 See G. W. Kuhrt, *Believing in Baptism* (London: Mowbrays, 1987), ch. 11 (pp. 161ff.).

13 ibid., pp. 76f.

14 See, e.g., Alister McGrath, *Understanding Doctrine* (London: Hodder & Stoughton, 1990), especially ch. 13.

15 See D. N. Bell, *A Cloud of Witnesses* (Kalamazoo, MI: Cistercian Publications, 1989) and Alister McGrath, *Understanding Jesus* (Eastbourne: Kingsway, 1987) or McGrath, *Understanding Doctrine*, especially ch. 11.

16 For a good introduction to the debate, see D. L. Edwards and J. R. W. Stott, *Essentials: A Liberal–Evangelical Dialogue* (London: Hodder & Stoughton, 1988), especially ch. 2.

17 See G. N. Stanton, *The Gospels and Jesus* (Oxford: Oxford University Press, 1989).

18 See J. R. W. Stott, *The Contemporary Christian* (Leicester: Inter-Varsity Press, 1992), pp. 337ff.

19 A. Schweitzer, *The Quest of the Historical Jesus* (ET: London, 1910).

20 C. H. Dodd, *The Parables of the Kingdom* (London: J. Nisbet & Co., 1935).

21 cf. Rom. 5:9–10, Col. 1:14 and Rom. 8:15 with Rom. 5:9–10 and 8:23.

22 Stott, *The Contemporary Christian*, pp. 377ff.

23 A. M. Ramsey, *The Christian Priest Today* (London: SPCK, 1985), p. 7.

Hodder Christian Paperbacks: a tradition of excellence.

Great names and great books to enrich your life and meet your needs. Choose from such authors as:

Corrie ten Boom	Jackie Pullinger
Charles Colson	David Pytches
Richard Foster	Mary Pytches
Billy Graham	Jennifer Rees Larcombe
Michael Green	Cliff Richard
Michele Guinness	John Stott
Joyce Huggett	Joni Eareckson Tada
Francis MacNutt	Colin Urquhart
Catherine Marshall	David Watson
Jim Packer	David Wilkerson
Adrian Plass	John Wimber

The wide range of books on the Hodder Christian Paperback list include **biography, personal testimony, devotional books, evangelistic books, christian teaching, fiction, drama, poetry, books that give help for times of need** – and many others.

Ask at your nearest Christian bookshop or at your church bookstall for the latest titles.

SOME BESTSELLERS IN HODDER CHRISTIAN PAPERBACKS

THE HIDING PLACE by Corrie ten Boom

The triumphant story of Corrie ten Boom, heroine of the anti-Nazi underground.

"A brave and heartening story."

Baptist Times

GOD'S SMUGGLER by Brother Andrew

An international bestseller. God's Smuggler carries contraband Bibles past armed border guards to bring the love of Christ to the people behind the Iron Curtain.

"A book you will not want to miss."

Catherine Marshall

DISCIPLESHIP by David Watson

". . . breath-taking, block-busting, Bible-based simplicity on every page."

Jim Packer

LISTENING TO GOD by Joyce Huggett

A profound spiritual testimony, and practical help for discovering a new dimension of prayer.

"This is counselling at its best."

Leadership Today

CELEBRATION OF DISCIPLINE by Richard Foster

A classic on the Spiritual Disciplines.

"For any Christian hungry for teaching, I would recommend this as being one of the most challenging books to have been published."

Delia Smith

RUN BABY RUN by Nicky Cruz with Jamie Buckingham

A tough New York gang leader discovers Christ.

"It is a thrilling story. My hope is that it shall have a wide reading."

Billy Graham

CHASING THE DRAGON by Jackie Pullinger with Andrew Quicke

Life-changing miracles in Hong Kong's Walled City.

"A book to stop you in your tracks."

Liverpool Daily Post

BORN AGAIN by Charles Colson

Disgraced by Watergate, Charles Colson finds a new life.

"An action packed story of real life drama and a revelation of modern history as well as a moving personal account."

Elim Evangel